MISSION:

BE A *KIND* MOSQUITO

Edited by	Abigail Prowse
Book cover	Jelena Mirkovic
Illustrations	Renata Galindo
Graphics Reproduction	Wilma Pedroza
Layout design	Olivier Darbonville

ISBN: 978-1-9196330-0-8

MISSION

BE A KIND MOSQUITO

A MANUAL FOR A HEALTHIER
WORLD AND A HAPPIER YOU

SOFIA PAVON

CONTENTS

AUTHOR'S NOTE

 If you think you are too small to make a difference, try sleeping with a mosquito.

— DALAI LAMA

I don't know what it is, exactly, that causes *THE* change. When do we stop thinking only about ourselves and our loved ones? When do we realize the extent to which the rest of the world's sentient beings are suffering? When do we start to feel compassion towards others? When do we become aware of the damage caused by our actions; aware of an urge to change? Maybe it is through the reading of a book, a random act of kindness, or the influence of a wise friend, or perhaps through a spiritual retreat. It is true that, in order to wake up to reality, one might need a powerful experience of great suffering, a terrible accident or illness, the loss of a loved one... Or it can happen merely by silencing the world around us and delving deeper into our soul. Suddenly, it is as if a veil has been lifted from our faces, and a new world has opened up before our eyes. A world that is more in line with reality – a glimpse beyond the self, the ego. A world where we can plainly see how much suffering could be avoided if we all did something about it.

Often, we move through our lives in a dream-like state, where we are encouraged to conform and behave like one another, never stopping to question whether we are acting ethically or not. We buy clothes made in factories where modern slaves work without any rights; we consume meat and dairy from factory farms where animals are abused and treated like machines; we use too many disposable products; we waste too much food; we always want more. We are consuming the earth's resources at a rapid pace, without considering sustainability and recovery. We simply fail to consider the consequences of our actions. We don't realize that every decision we make has a consequence – be it for better or for worse.

Together, overpopulation, ignorance, and greed for money and power have led the world to forget about the basic principles and values essential to sustaining life. But how do we free ourselves and remove the blindfold? What causes *the change?*

This book is not intended to criticize everything we do or don't do; it is merely an encounter with our conscience. It is a wake-up call aimed at preventing us from living a life void of awareness or true meaning. The purpose is to help us discover ourselves as unique and powerful individuals, to inform the reader of the destruction that we are causing to our world. This book aims to explore the threats and dangers in existence now, to create awareness of the consequences of our every action, and – most importantly – to trigger a new initiative within all of us. This initiative urges us to demonstrate the power that we have as individuals to change things for the better, before it is too late. By creating awareness, we will develop compassion, and this compassion will be the engine that drives collective change.

One evening, an old Cherokee was teaching his grandson about the battle that goes on inside us all:

"There is a fight between two wolves going on inside each of us," he said to the boy. "One is evil – he is greed, anger, envy, sorrow, regret, guilt, arrogance, self-pity, resentment, inferiority, lies, false pride, superiority, and ego. The other is good – he is generosity, compassion, joy, peace, love, hope, serenity, humility, kindness, benevolence, empathy, truth, and faith."

The grandson thought about it for a minute, and then asked his grandfather, "Which wolf will win?" and the grandfather simply replied, "The one you feed."

(A CHEROKEE LEGEND)

INTRODUCTION

Upon the conduct of each
depends the fate of all.

— ALEXANDER THE GREAT

When I reflect upon myself, I feel a little ashamed of some of my past actions and decisions. Not that I was a terrible person, but I just failed to realize the weight and the importance of my behavior upon my surroundings. I was not thinking for myself; I was simply following the path of the masses, without ever questioning why. Then, at some point in my life, something changed inside me. Compassion took over my heart in a truly painful way. At once, I suddenly began to investigate my self-centered past: one in which I was unaware of the pain and suffering that my actions caused to others, living in an egocentric and selfish manner, letting each day pass without doing anything truly profound for myself or for others. One of the first drastic changes that this brought was my reaction to the news: my heart ached watching the floods of 'undesired' immigrants constantly turned away from borders, or the children in extreme poverty dying of preventable illnesses. I was outraged by the inequalities around the world, the pain that animals endure for our pleasure, and the destruction that we are causing to the planet. I was no longer indifferent. I wanted to do something about it.

What I learned with this sudden experience is that every person has the potential to do good, to do evil, or just to live a hollow life without substantial meaning. It all depends on how closely we are able to see reality as it really is, and how much we hold our hearts open when we experience this reality.

From the moment we are born, the countdown of our LIFE starts. In other words, we start to die. Even if we would prefer to forget about it, death is an intrinsic part of everything. Poor and rich, beautiful and ugly, we all end up the same way. The money, the 'things' that we cherish so dearly, the power and fame, will no longer matter at the time of our death. Only our actions through the course of our life will be of importance: the love and care that we gave to others, the help and concern towards the pain and suffering that crossed our path, and the respect we showed towards all forms of life. A life lived with a kind heart is the only way to experience a peaceful death, without regret.

It is vital to understand that every single one of our actions has an impact on the world. If we behave morally, wisely, and responsibly in our lives, if we act with a compassionate heart towards all forms of life, all the connections around us will be positively affected. On the contrary, if our decisions are based on greed, selfishness, or ignorance, this will come back to harm us. We have much more power than we believe. Think about all the people that we encounter every day. Every person that crosses our path has an opportunity to affect us, just as we have an opportunity to affect them - be it for good or bad. Our daily habits and actions have a direct impact on nature, and on the lives of people and animals around the world. For this reason, we have to be active, compassionate participants of society, for the future of humanity.

Unfortunately, it seems that materialism, power and greed have taken over the world - now more than ever. Whilst the post-industrial era brought commodities and inventions that made life simpler, it also brought a gradual loss of ethics and principles, and the erosion of personal values. This accelerated lifestyle, coupled with an accessibility to material goods, made life more superfluous and devoid of real meaning (and of kinder hearts).

Many of the public services and economic systems currently in place (e.g., energy supplies, certain areas of the medical system, the industrial production of food) are neither efficient nor beneficial. Rather than focusing upon the wellbeing of their consumers (and of the planet), they are more focused on the wealth and power of the industries that provide for them. In all these fields, it seems evident that there is a lack of ethics and global social justice, a lack of compassion and love for others. We have this view of the world where our personal wellbeing is at the center of importance, even if it comes at a cost to others. We harbor a belief that everything that exists on Earth is for our use and at our disposal... But it is important to understand that we are all so interconnected that our wellbeing is directly dependent on the wellbeing of others. If we act and make decisions with a selfish and narrow mind, we will be directly affected by the consequences.

This can be seen in the way we have been treating the planet. We have not taken nature and the environment into consideration when employing new technologies. We are drying out the earth as if its resources are inexhaustible – but they are not. And the results are out there now. We share this planet with many other forms of life which we must acknowledge and respect. The earth is not ours; we are its guests. We must understand that we humans are not perfect, but nature is. Respecting the laws of nature and all forms of life within it will always bring positive effects. But if we go against it, we will see devastating results in no time; these effects are already beginning to show.

It is difficult to find clarity in a society filled with irrelevant and contradictory information. In my opinion, this may be a main factor contributing to the lack of action taken by the average citizen. We are too busy living our lives, trying to survive in a chaotic world, blindly trusting the news that comes our way. We do not seem to notice the worrying picture of everything that is starting to happen due to human actions; we do not make the connection that the floods, the record heat waves, or any other extreme changes in weather are consequences of these actions, caused by a lack of human understanding. Unfortunately, we as a society still trust the information provided to us by leaders, many of whom still don't even believe in climate change and see this extreme phenomenon as merely a collection of exceptional cases. We still trust that everybody is responsible and honest, and we wait patiently for them to act and take the necessary measures at some point. But this is not happening. It is time to wake up to reality; to stop being naive and passive. The drastic actions needed for the planet's survival are not being treated as a priority, and the earth is degrading more and more every day. We must act now; we have to inform ourselves of the situation and find out which actions need to be taken. We are on the verge of reaching a point of no return in terms of the destruction of the planet. It may feel overwhelming to think of everything that humankind needs to do in order to recover a little bit of sanity, and to start taking vital measures to undo the damage. But the solutions are within reach. The problem is that many of our priorities are wrongly skewed. It is our turn to act and to urge leaders, to join the Pacific Revolution for a higher good – even if this means civil disobedience.

We must reconsider our values and live with a higher ethical code. We must respect all kinds of life, for we don't have any right to abuse our superiority and inflict pain. We need to wake up and see the suffering that we are all causing, and start making decisions based on the wellbeing of humanity. Wishing for and working towards happiness for all living beings will automatically bring happiness and wellbeing to us as humans.

Be a Kind Mosquito is nothing more than an encounter with our own conscience. It is a wake-up call aimed at preventing us from living a life void of awareness and true meaning. It informs its readers about the destruction that we are causing to our world, exploring the present threats and dangers to existence, and creates awareness of the consequences of our every action. Its purpose is to help us discover ourselves as unique individuals, capable of instigating change. Perhaps most importantly, its aim is to trigger a new initiative within all of us to demonstrate the power that we all possess to change things for the better, before it is too late.

01

ON NATURE AND ITS THREADS. THE PROBLEMS.

 A human being is a part of the whole called by us 'Universe', a part limited in time and space. He experiences himself, his thoughts and feelings, as something separated from the rest, a kind of optical delusion of his consciousness. This delusion is a kind of prison for us, restricting us to our personal desires and to affection for a few persons nearest to us. Our task must be to free ourselves from this prison by widening our circle of compassion to embrace all living creatures and the whole of nature in its beauty.

— ALBERT EINSTEIN

1.1 The Fragility of the Ecosystem

It was with great joy that I came across the book *The Secret Network of Nature* by Peter Wohlleben[1] - a work full of knowledge and wisdom about the natural world. One of the main lessons this book offers its reader is the understanding that every creature, from the tiny insect to larger animals and trees, has a purpose on Earth. Wohlleben tells countless enthralling stories which define the perfection of nature: trees, for instance, have been found to communicate and share nutrients with each other via their roots. They protect their siblings and have the power to make their leaves taste bad for predators. Ravens and wolves also have a deal: when wolves are eating their prey, ravens alert them to any danger when a bear or other predator is approaching from afar. In return, wolves allow ravens to enjoy a share of the prize. Wolf cubs have been spotted playing with ravens, so ravens are considered by wolves as part of their community.

Now let's consider salmon. These majestic heroes are key for the survival of the forests and its inhabitants. They are born in streams and rivers, and then migrate to live their adult life in sea waters. When they are ready to reproduce, they battle their way hundreds of miles back to their natal rivers, avoiding predators and fighting their way upstream, with the sole purpose of spawning in those familiar waters. When they arrive, they use their last ounce of strength to mate and then, exhausted, they die. Since salmon migrate en masse, there is a feast waiting for hungry bears, who will drag their catch far into the forest to enjoy it in peace. After eating mainly the fatty parts of the fish, they will leave the rest to other forest animals, like foxes, birds of prey and innumerable quantities of insects, which will further distribute all the nutrients contained in the salmon, such as nitrogen and phosphorus. The remaining parts of this precious fish, plus the feces of the feasting animals, will then be absorbed to fertilize the soil.[2]

These examples represent the fragility and the interconnectedness of the earth's ecosystems. Nature is a complicated mechanism, where every piece is essential for the others to function correctly. Any modification or transformation of this delicate system may alter its entire structure and operation.

1.2 Global Interconnection.

In this interconnected world, everything that exists, no matter how small, plays its role in the survival of the earth. Humankind is just a small part of this cycle. There is a perfect balance in the earth's ecosystems that allow every sentient being to live and contribute to this balance. But we are the only sentient being not doing our part. Even worse, we are the ones rapidly altering this delicate balance.

We tend to perceive the world as being independent from ourselves, but it is crucial to understand that we are all connected, just as everything in nature is connected back to us. When human activity disturbs one part of an ecosystem, the consequences will extend much further than one may suspect. Let's take deforestation, for instance: one of the consequences of the mass destruction of forests is the instigation of floods in several parts of the world. Trees absorb large amounts of water in their trunks and branches, protecting the soil from eroding, and recharging and purifying the groundwater supply. By preventing erosion, forests inhibit surface run-off, which decreases the risk of flooding. Via plant transpiration, forests transport these large quantities of water into the atmosphere, replenishing clouds of water through the prompting of rainfall, which refills lakes and rivers.

Trees are also great air purifiers. By absorbing large amounts of toxic chemicals produced by pollution through their leaves, they purify the air we breathe, transforming toxins into oxygen. When we destroy a forest, we are not just destroying the trees which are vital to our survival, but are also destroying the whole ecosystem within them. We are eliminating all the living creatures which depend on those forests, and which play a major role in the equilibrium of the earth. By destroying an ecosystem, dependent species are not able to reproduce anymore, as the environment has become unsafe for them and their offspring, who are unable to find food for themselves. This is one of the reasons why so many species are in danger of disappearing from our planet, why there has been an alarming decline in insects and vertebrates, and why there is an increased warming of the earth's temperature. We will later explore the primary causes of this alarming decline.

Powerful Humans with Limited Wisdom

 Water and air, the two essential fluids
on which all life depends, have become
global garbage cans.

- JACQUES-YVES COUSTEAU

Unfortunately, man is far from perfect. Nature provides human beings with all the potential for perfection, but the cultural influences which we receive whilst growing up often tarnish our minds. The society that we have created spoils the true self. Many young children, for instance, would naturally refuse to eat meat when they come to understand that it is the result of killing an animal, which they often consider a friend.

From the moment we are born, we are bombarded with contradictory information about life that makes us lose sight of the truth. Most of the time, the education that we receive is based on the idea that we are the most important beings in the world, and that all our actions must be based on our own personal wellbeing, looking at others as competitors, rather than part of the same humanity. Hence the results.

By concentrating on our own needs whilst neglecting the needs of the earth and other forms of life, we are breaking down its ecosystems and consuming its resources at a worrying pace. The crude reality is that the earth does not need humans. In fact, without us, nature would flourish. But we can live together in harmony if we simply find greener solutions for our needs.

According to the scientific community, we have entered a new geological era known as the Anthropocene Age, where human actions have caused imbalances and destruction in terrestrial and marine ecosystems, among many other consequences. One of the main characteristics of this era is the urge to have too much. Nothing can satiate our appetite to have more, and more, and more. Be it more clothing, more cosmetics, a better car, a larger home, or other things that, most of the time, we do not need. This accumulation of useless possessions, as well as a loss of connection with nature, is making us lose touch with reality. Just a few decades ago, children would spend most of their free time outside, watching ants at work, making castles out of dirt, jumping in puddles, or climbing enormous trees. This is not the case anymore for most children living in developed countries. Technology and social media have replaced the invaluable experience of spending time outdoors. Sadly, children as young as three or four years old are now using electronic devices, steering them even further away from reality.

When we promote contact with nature in our children's lives, we are offering a gift that will last a lifetime. It is a wise approach to make them understand and respect nature and its sacred balance. In a 2019 study by Myriam Preuss et al, published in the *International Journal of Environment Research and Public Health,* (*Low Childhood Nature Exposure Is Associated with Worse Mental Health in Adulthood*), adults who experienced low levels of natural outdoor environmental exposure in childhood reported significantly worse mental health when compared to adults with high levels of childhood nature exposure.[3] The study was based on data from 2585 participants between 18-75 years old. It was also identified that low levels of nature exposure in childhood were associated with a lower perceived importance of natural outdoor environments, meaning that the interest in spending time in these natural environments decreases.[4]

Birds and Butterflies

I have a very clear and happy memory from my childhood, in which I would be woken up every morning by the sound of birds. There were so many of them! My bedroom window was just in front of a large palm tree, where birds loved to gather at dawn. They were my alarm clock, and I always woke up naturally, feeling well-rested.

Over the past several years, I have noticed that I can no longer hear many birds singing. I have observed a worrying decrease of birds, butterflies, and all flying beings. Thirty years ago, there was not one day that passed without seeing a butterfly. Meadows and fields were covered with these delicate and stunning creatures. Nowadays, they have become so rare that seeing them brings surprise. Then I came across the 2020 WWF Biennial living planet report (the non-profit international wildlife conservation) and read a worrying fact: the study reveals that the vertebrate population (birds, mammals, fish, amphibians and reptiles) has fallen by an average of 68% globally since 1970 – more than two thirds in less than 50 years![5] Furthermore, a recent study performed in 60 protected areas in Germany suggests that there has been a decline in flying insects of more than 75% over almost 30 years. This includes butterflies, bees, dragonflies, etc., with a 41% decrease in just the last decade.

In a 2018 study led by the Xerces Society for invertebrate conservation, the California Monarch butterfly population was found to have decreased by 86% when compared to 2017. In this same way, many other species are on the brink of extinction.[6] Since birds feed mainly upon insects, this decline in the insect population is directly related to the birds' decline. Because, as we have seen repeatedly, everything is connected.

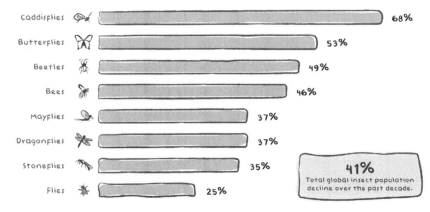

MASSIVE INSECT DECLINE THREATENS COLLAPSE OF NATURE

Percentage decline in selected global insect populations over the past decade.

Insect	Decline
Caddisflies	68%
Butterflies	53%
Beetles	49%
Bees	46%
Mayflies	37%
Dragonflies	37%
Stoneflies	35%
Flies	25%

41% Total global insect population decline over the past decade.

Source: Sánchez-Bayo & Wyckhuys, Biological Conservation, 2019.

We must save wildlife: not just because it makes us happy, not just because it reduces stress, or because it is a beautiful sight to see. We need to save it because human beings need wildlife to survive. Honeybees, for instance, carry out around 80% of all pollination worldwide. Without pollinators, humankind and all life on Earth could not survive. By carrying pollen from one flower to another, pollinators secure the production of seeds, which ensures a new generation of plants. Flowers, fruits, vegetables, and grains rely on the presence of pollinators to reproduce.

VULNERABLE VERTEBRATES

Earth's vertebrate populations declined by 58% between 1970 and 2012, with human activities much to blame.

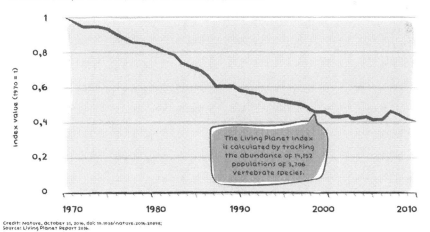

The Living Planet Index is calculated by tracking the abundance of 14,152 populations of 3,706 vertebrate species.

Credit: Nature, October 31, 2016, doi: 10.1038/nature.2016.20898;
Source: Living Planet Report 2016.

When we hear of news like this, we might think that it is out of our hands; that we could never do something big enough to make a change. But that is far from true. When we understand the causes of this decline, we can make small changes in our everyday lives that will make an impact. As we will discuss later, if we all work together, we can make a change, and do our very best to reverse the damage caused.

1.3 Climate Change. Is it Real?

 Any attempt to solve the ecological crisis within a bourgeois framework must be dismissed as chimerical. Capitalism is inherently anti-ecological. Competition and accumulation constitute its very law of life, a law... summarized in the phrase, 'production for the sake of production.' Anything, however hallowed or rare, 'has its price' and is fair game for the marketplace. In a society of this kind, nature is necessarily treated as a mere resource to be plundered and exploited. The destruction of the natural world, far being the result of mere hubristic blunders, follows inexorably from the very logic of capitalist production.

-MURRAY BOOKCHIN

GLOBAL REPORTED NATURAL DISASTERS BY TYPE

The annual reported number of natural disasters, categorised by type. This includes both weather and non-weather related disasters.

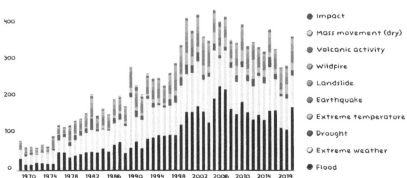

Source: EMDAT (2020): OFDA/CRED International Disaster Database, Université Catholique de Louvain - Brussels - Belgium. OurWorldInData.org/natural-disasters . CC BY

Climate change is real: there is no doubt about it. Our planet is warming up at an accelerated pace. The poles are melting, putting countless species at risk of extinction, such as penguins and polar bears, and causing the ocean to acidify. This "ocean acidification" negatively affects marine organisms, which are a vital part of the food chain. The effects of this are becoming more evident with each year that passes without any action towards change.

The extreme weather changes that have been occurring over the past decade, and the devastating harm that comes with them, are increasing in both intensity and frequency. These will only continue to rise if nothing is done to reverse – or at least stop – this destructive cycle; there will be more rainfall, followed by longer and drier droughts, the storms and floods will become stronger and deadlier. Hurricanes, tsunamis, and earthquakes will also become more frequent.[7]

Developed countries are the major culprits in this equation, but the populations in developing countries are often the ones suffering the worst consequences, making climate change the biggest social injustice of the modern era. By experiencing a naturally warmer climate, these nations are drastically affected by the rise of temperatures. Agriculture, for instance, is severely damaged, increasing extreme poverty and world hunger. As the earth warms up, disease-carrying mosquitoes are able to survive in temperate parts of the world, extending illnesses such as malaria and dengue fever beyond their current habitat. Without the means for research and technology, governments in these countries will not be able to find solutions for the problems that are growing in intensity.

Regrettably, some leaders still deny this reality, and quote the earth's natural cycle as the culprit of these changes, continuing to cause harm with their polluting policies. It is true that there have been swings of temperature in the planet's history. This is a normal phenomenon that occurs naturally on the planet, but the pace of this occurrence is naturally extremely slow and steady. Since the Industrial Revolution, the warming of the earth has accelerated at an alarmingly unnatural pace; there is no doubt about this for scientists all over the world. This uncontrolled global warming is due to human activity.[8]

~~~~~~

The Industrial Revolution brought with it massive developments in science and technology, whilst, the world's population began to experience major growth. With the appearance of factories, the costs of products decreased. At the same time, with the advances in medicine, general health improved. Together, this allowed the population a better quality of life, which in turn enabled them to marry younger and have more children.

~~~~~~

While this progress brought countless advantages to society in general, it also came with detrimental consequences for nature - consequences that have not stopped growing in severity since then. The excess level of greenhouse gases generated by human activities such as transportation and manufacturing, alongside the tremendous production of food needed to feed an ever-growing population, are causing extensive deforestation, sparking a negative impact on our planet that has become increasingly severe.

One of the reasons that governments, and society in general, do not take sufficient action in terms of reverting this alarming situation may be that the disturbing effects of climate change are not easily evident at first glance. We are used to acting on immediate urges: on visible threats to our wellbeing which we can remediate and see results instantly. We are not good at acting towards not-so-palpable negative situations, where the results of our actions are more noticeable after a longer period of time. If society does not feel directly affected by a problem, it is harder to make them act responsibly and initiate preventive measures, just as it is difficult to make them understand the real danger that draws closer every day.

I think the changes that have occurred as a result of climate change are better seen by older generations, who experienced a world with purer air, more wildlife, larger quantities of birds and butterflies, virgin forests, more stable weather, and tastier fruits, vegetables, bread and grains. Yes, the causes of climate change also affect the quality of our food; the mass production of food in industrial agricultural practices sacrifices quality for quantity. But sadly, and shamefully, although the damage being done to our planet is more evident for the older generation, they are not the ones pushing for change. It is the younger generations who are actively moving and pressuring governments to put greener policies into place.

I often wonder what would happen if our leaders took the same urgent actions towards climate change as they did towards avoiding the spread of the COVID-19 pandemic, for which they put in place strict and immediate measures with the purpose of controlling the number of deaths. However, the accelerated heating of our planet is also causing deaths on a mass scale. Experts estimate that climate change is already causing over 150,000 deaths annually by severe weather events such as hurricanes, fires, and flooding, and this will continue to grow if no changes are made. According to a 2018 report from the World Health Organization, global warming would cause an additional 250,000 deaths per year due to malnutrition, heat stress, malaria and diarrhea.[9] Note that this only concerns human deaths, without even beginning to consider the enormous loss of wildlife habitats and the extinction of species.

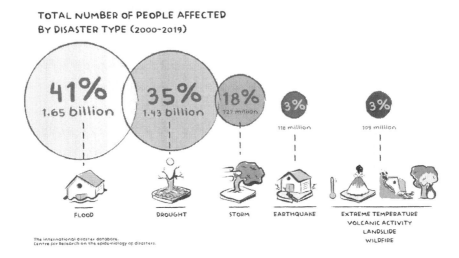

TOTAL NUMBER OF PEOPLE AFFECTED
BY DISASTER TYPE (2000-2019)

41%
1.65 billion

35%
1.43 billion

18%
727 million

3%
118 million

3%
109 million

FLOOD   DROUGHT   STORM   EARTHQUAKE   EXTREME TEMPERATURE
VOLCANIC ACTIVITY
LANDSLIDE
WILDFIRE

The international disaster database.
Centre for Research on the epidemiology of disasters.

If we don't act now, the outlook for the future is worrying. Over time, economies will be destabilized and people in poorer countries will not be able to cope with the climate crisis. This alone should be a good enough reason to act immediately. But this is not all. Although pandemics have been present throughout history, there is no doubt that the destruction of ecosystems raises the risk of the frequency and seriousness of them. In an article from the New York Times, *We Made the Coronavirus Epidemic* by David Quammen, author of *Spillover: Animal Infections and the Next Human Pandemic* shows how human actions are causing the emergence of deadly pandemics such as COVID-19 and Ebola. *"We invade tropical forests and other wild landscapes, which harbor so many species of animals and plants — and within those creatures, so many unknown viruses. We cut the trees; we kill the animals or cage them and send them to markets. We disrupt ecosystems, and we shake viruses loose from their natural hosts. When that happens, they need a new host. Often, we are it."*[10] But even though scientists and experts have been warning about the connection between pandemics and the warming of the earth, we still are not acting as urgently as we should. We are choosing to control the pandemic with face masks and gloves, rather than changing our way of living. Our leaders would rather concentrate all their efforts onto finding a vaccine than attacking the real source of the crisis. It is like putting a Band-Aid on a critical wound.

1.4 Can We Trust our Leaders?

 Already, 2020's might-have-beens are fading into history, another year when political and corporate leaders failed to meet the moment's demands. We know temperatures will keep climbing, not-so-natural disasters will keep coming and the need for swift action will only increase. All is not lost, and there is progress to build on — new promises nations and companies must be held to, clean power that's cheaper and more reliable than our dirty, old fuels, and the urgency that rises as the terrible reality of climate change becomes ever more apparent.

- BETH GARDINER (AUTHOR)

Because the consequences of climate change are growing at such a rapid pace, there is a real urge to act now. Whilst some governments are making important changes in their policies, the larger countries that could make the most noticeable positive effect on the planet are, unfortunately, running out of precious time. China and the USA are at the top of this list as the major producers of greenhouse gases, but despite this, they are not considering the urgency of the situation, and are not addressing their responsibility in the warming of the planet. When Trump was in power, he made detrimental decisions that caused further destruction of the environment. One of the first things that ex-president Trump did when entering office was to announce his plans to withdraw from the Paris Climate Agreement: one of the major global agreements within the UN between 197 countries. This alliance focuses largely on the reduction of greenhouse gas emissions, among other issues. Its aim is to hold rising temperatures to "well below 2°C above pre-industrial levels by the end of the century."

But this was not the only decision against the environment made by Trump. He also opened public land for mining and drilling; he modified the Endangered Species Act and the Migratory Bird Treaty Act by tipping the balance towards economic considerations, rather than the protection of birds and endangered species; he issued an executive order which called for a sharp logging increase on public land. These are just a few of the many other policies that his government established which prioritized "business as usual", as if the global emergency were inexistent. Trump's anti-science view of reality made the USA one of the most dangerous and irresponsible polluter countries in the world.[11] Fortunately for the world, Mr. Trump did not last long; now it is up to President Joe Biden to recover those four years of detrimental decisions, and to start acting in favour of the planet and all life upon it. This, he is already doing: the first step that he took upon entering office was to return the US to the Paris Climate Agreement.

As the world's major producer of greenhouse gases (many of these emissions are also caused by the exportation of goods to the USA), China is similarly not doing enough to keep the rising temperature levels below the Paris Agreement's long-term goal of 1.5°C. Their efforts have been rated by officials as highly insufficient.[12] The consumption of fossil fuels has been increasing over the past few years, which is inconsistent with the terms of the Paris Agreement. It can be argued that China's President Xi Jinping has been taking important pro-environmental steps towards a greener nation, but unfortunately this has not extended outside their immediate country. Overseas, China has become one of the world's largest builders and providers of coal power plants. So, is President Jinping truly worried about the environment, or is he just playing politics?

Although Brazil is not classed as one of the top greenhouse gas emitters, it holds 64% of the major lung of the earth: the Amazon Rainforest.

Sadly, the destruction of this vital resource has increased at a rapid pace since the nation's new far-right president stepped in. Since his election, President Bolsonaro has formally opened protected areas of the Amazon for commercial exploitation. Mr. Bolsonaro's administration cut the main environmental agency's budget by 24%. Just after seven months into his term, the Amazon had already lost more than 1,330 square miles of forest cover.[13] Bolsonaro's irresponsibility does not just end with the destruction of the Amazon; he has also turned a blind eye to criminal activity against the indigenous people that have been trying to defend the rainforest themselves, following a lack of law enforcement. These groups have been threatened, attacked, and, according to community leaders, murdered by the people engaged in this devastating destruction.[14]

If this were not enough, the Amazon has also suffered extensive deforestation due to the production of soy. This is mainly caused by the substantial levels of soy exportation to China, making both countries responsible for this wreckage.

We cannot leave the future of our planet in the hands of the few that control it now. So far, we have seen how governments and big industries prioritize monetary interests over the planet, so now it is up to us to act. We must pressure our leaders; we have to take action. We have a responsibility towards future generations and the other beings that share this earth with us. Those of us living in high income, first-world countries have an even greater responsibility, since these countries have a much larger carbon footprint than lower income nations. Every one of us can play a part in protecting the earth. We will soon discover how.

1.5 Knowing the Main Culprits

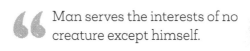 Man serves the interests of no creature except himself.

– GEORGE ORWELL

1) Burning of Fossil Fuels.

There are two main categories of resources which produce energy: renewable and non-renewable.

Renewable energy derives from natural sources, and regenerates itself continually, meaning that it is practically inexhaustible. Examples of renewable energy sources are solar energy, hydropower, and wind. These sources have a very low environmental impact.

Non-renewable energy sources diminish over time and are not able to replenish themselves. Because of this, additional resources are needed for their regeneration, which takes a very long time. The production of non-renewable energy causes a major impact upon the environment and contributes to pollution and the exhaustion of Earth's natural resources.

Most of the greenhouse gases responsible for the warming of the earth come from the combustion of non-renewable fossil fuels, such as natural gas and coal. These gases are used mainly for electricity, heat, and transportation. Non-renewable fuels such as these are extracted from the earth and, when burned, release carbon dioxide among other greenhouse gases; these cause heat to become trapped in the earth's atmosphere. Developed countries have been burning fossil fuels since the Industrial Revolution, and this is one of the reasons that these countries are richer and more prosperous than the rest of the world. Now would be the time to allow developing countries to burn these fuels for their own development and prosperity. Unfortunately, if we want to maintain the livability of our planet, this is not an option. Since the warming of the earth is mainly due to the fossil fuel extraction of powerful countries, it is time for these richer countries to find sustainable ways to provide energy, whilst at the same time supporting the rest of the world in their development via greener and more sustainable energy generation options. These could be in the form of solar panels, wind turbines, or prioritizing investments in research for cleaner energy. Even nuclear power may be a less harmful option for the planet than coal extraction; but after the Chernobyl and the Fukushima disasters, there is deep-rooted feeling of distrust in society for this method of energy generation.

It is true that nuclear accidents are catastrophic, but they are rare. Under ideal conditions, a nuclear power plant is safe, and does not contribute to climate change, since it does not emit toxic gases, unlike the use of coal. The risk still exists, so renewables are and will always be the safest option for all.

The problem is that there are many financial and materialistic interests involved in the gas, oil, and coal industry, and as a consequence, very little effort or constraint has been invested into establishing a more energy-efficient, climate-friendly solution. Even with treaties like the Paris Agreement, the results have been deceiving. This is mainly because the sanctions for failure to fulfill the targets are mild or inexistent. At least now the USA, which is the country most responsible for the warming of our planet, (since much of the warming activity produced by China is for USA exports) has rejoined the accord. What will it take for our leaders to understand that we are running out of time? An immediate stop to fossil fuel extraction is no longer an option but a *requirement* to saving the planet, and, in turn, to saving us all.

Scientists from all over the world agree on the urgency to act. According to German atmospheric physicist Hans Joachim Schellnhuber, "I would like people to panic and take action according to the state of emergency we are in." As also stated by the founder and now director emeritus of the Potsdam Climate Institute, *"people who turn a blind eye to Climate Change remind me of the joke about the man falling from the Empire State Building saying "So far everything is OK."*

"

People who turn a blind eye to Climate Change remind me of the joke about the man falling from the Empire State Building saying 'So far everything is OK.'

2) Agriculture

 It is impossible to have a healthy and sound society without the proper respect for the soil.

– PETER MAURIN

One of the major challenges in society is finding a sustainable food system to feed the incessantly increasing population, whilst at the same time finding a way to protect the planet.

Agriculture has changed a great deal in the last few decades. Not so long ago, a large percentage of society's activity was related to farming. These farmers would provide food to local residents whilst farm animals which lived in humanely raised conditions, grassing freely in the fields, provided healthy and nutritious produce for its consumers. Animal manure would help the soil gain all the necessary nutrients for producing healthy crops. There were no antibiotics given to farm animals. The pesticides used in the fields were relatively mild and never excessive; this same concept applied to the tillage used in the land. There was no need to move produce from one place to another. It was a healthy, locally-focused system. None of this is the reality now. Be it due to the Industrial Revolution, the growing population, or the power that the large industrial agriculture companies have acquired, the well-balanced system of the past has fallen through. Here is the current situation of the origins of our food:

CROP FIELDS

With a high demand of food needed to feed the growing population, we have begun to lose the artisan touch. Large-scale farms, where mass production is the goal, began to replace small, local farmers. Nowadays, most of our food comes from these industrial farms. In order to have better control over the fields, these farms repetitively harvest a single crop (monocropping), using a significant amount of highly toxic pesticides - some of which have been linked to many illnesses, including Parkinson's disease, diabetes, and cancer.[15] As weeds became increasingly resistant to these chemicals, more and more pesticides were required to keep fields weed- and pest-free. In order to control this situation, Genetically Modified Organisms (GMO) were created by biotech giant Monsanto (now part of Bayer). GMOs (also known as Genetically Engineered [GE] and Biotechnology-Derived [BD]) are organisms (e.g., corn or soybean seeds) in which the genetic material (DNA) has been altered using genetic engineering techniques, with the purpose of making them herbicide-tolerant. This way, it is possible to use large

amounts of highly toxic herbicides such as Glyphosate (e.g., Roundup) in crop fields, killing all types of herbs, pests, and vegetation, with only the altered organism surviving.

Theoretically, the initial purpose of GMO crops was to improve the protection of plants against pests and viruses, thus increasing food production. But after more than twenty years of use, it seems that they have not served their purpose as expected. During all these years of intensive farming methods, there has been an alarming depletion of nutrients in soils where these transgenic crops are grown; lifeless fields are left behind where nothing else can survive. According to a 2004 study published in the *Journal of the American College of Nutrition* by researcher Donald Davis and his team from the University of Texas (UT), there has been a significant decline in the amount of nutrients found in conventionally-grown fruits and vegetables over the past half century. Similar results have been found in the United Kingdom by nutritionist David Thomas (*Sage journal, Nutrition and Health, A Study on the Mineral Depletion of the Foods Available to us as a Nation over the Period 1940 to 1991*, David Thomas, First Published April 1, 2003). Both researchers agree on soil depletion as one of the main culprits. The intensive use of pesticides like Roundup turns the fields sterile, and crops grown in sterile soil lose most of their vital nutrients.[16] There are several studies that reveal the relationship between the use of pesticides like Glyphosate and a dramatic drop in soil fertility.[17] [18]The use of large amounts of Glyphosate is collapsing the microbe system, which is

essential to healthy soil. Microbes like bacteria and fungi are of vital importance for plant health. The sum of the various microorganisms living in a patch of land benefit plant growth by providing a series of nutrients, and even by suppressing root pathogens.

Another downside to the use of Glyphosate is that it has the potential to breed superweeds, which, in turn, need even stronger pesticides to kill them; here, a vicious cycle starts to form.

Even though the FDA has classified Roundup use as relatively safe, studies have shown a link between Glyphosate pesticide and damage to human cells, particularly in fetuses, even in very dilute formulations.[19]

When discussing the safety of these transgenic plants, there has been misleading information published, causing consumers to believe that GMOs are safe, when the reality is that there is not sufficient evidence about the effects of these artificial plants on human health. According to Jonathan R. Latham, Co-Founder and Executive Director of the Bioscience Resource Project, scientific tests on the safety of GMOs are "*often missing, procedures and reagents are badly described, and the results are often ambiguous or uninterpretable.*" After exposing several studies about the dangers of GMOs, Doctor Latham continues: "*Aside from grave doubts about the quality and integrity of risk assessments, I also have specific science-based concerns over GMOs. These concerns are mostly particular to specific transgenes and traits.*"[20]

The use of Glyphosate, however, has already been classified in 2015 by the International Agency for Research on Cancer as "*probably carcinogenic to humans*"; but this doesn't seem to be enough for many leaders to ban this dangerous pesticide.[21]

Some studies have exposed equally-worrying results. In an article from the American Academy of Environmental Medicine, the authors addressed the strong association between genetically modified foods and diseases in several animal studies. These include, but are not limited to: altered function of the liver, immune system dysregulation, infertility, negative alterations in the kidneys, pancreas and spleen, among many other ailments.[22]

These results should not be surprising. Who on earth would trust such an unethical company that has been making killer products since its conception? Monsanto was the creator of carcinogens, pesticides, and herbicides used in the past that have now been outlawed, such as Agent Orange and insecticide DDT; products that have also caused congenital malformations in children.[23] Appallingly enough, they have often been aware of the dangers that these chemicals were posing to our health, choosing to ignore the data and sacrifice many lives, merely for profit.[24] Furthermore, Monsanto imposes contracts to farmers, forbidding them from saving seeds year to year, in order to maximize its profits. Every year, they demand that farmers buy new, expensive seeds, squeezing their profits even further, and driving the farmers to bankruptcy; if they don't follow the company's rules, they must be prepared to face a lawsuit.

Genetically engineered crops were initially created to combat world hunger, but based on a report from 2009 by the Union of Concerned Scientists (UCS), it has failed to do so. "Failure to yield" reviewed two dozen academic studies and came to the conclusion that genetic engineering has failed to significantly increase US crop yields, despite two decades of research and 13 years of commercialization. *"If we are going to make headway in combating hunger due to overpopulation and climate change, we will need to increase crop yields: traditional breeding outperforms genetic engineering hands down,"* is the conclusion of the report.[25]

In a 2014 article written by director of the Institute for Social Ecology and author of various books about the environment Brian Tokar, he presents extensive evidence on how GMOs are not a solution for world hunger. *"Despite overwhelming evidence to the contrary, proponents of genetic engineering continue to assert that GMO research is essential to feeding the world's hungry in an increasingly uncertain and unstable climate."* He argues that the benefits derived from far less invasive innovations in agriculture are wider, and concludes:

"After more than 20 years of research and development, GMOs continue to present far more problems than benefits, and most of the purported advantages have proved limited at best; many simply do not withstand scientific scrutiny. Perhaps it is time to put this inherently problematic and invasive technology aside and instead redouble efforts around the world to advance far more benign and sustainable ways to improve the quality and availability of our food."

THE GMO THREAT TO FOOD SOVEREIGNTY:
SCIENCE, RESISTANCE AND TRANSFORMATION, BRIAN TOKAR.[26]

British writer for the *Guardian*, and author of several successful books, no one is better equipped than George Monbiot to explain our blindness in the face of world hunger. He also discusses the way members of the biotech industry like Monsanto have become more of a hindrance for farmers:

"The world has a surplus of food, but still people go hungry. They go hungry because they cannot afford to buy it. They cannot afford to buy it because the sources of wealth and the means of production have been captured and, in some cases, monopolized by landowners and corporations. The purpose of the biotech industry is to capture and monopolize the sources of wealth and the means of production ...

GM technology permits companies to ensure that everything we eat is owned by them. They can patent the seeds and the processes which give rise to them. They can make sure that crops can't be grown without their patented chemicals. They can prevent seeds from reproducing themselves. By buying up competing seed companies and closing them down, they can capture the food market, the biggest and most diverse market of all.

No one in her right mind would welcome this, so the corporations must persuade us to focus on something else ... We are told that ... by refusing to eat GM products, we are threatening the developing world with starvation, an argument that is, shall we say, imaginative ..."

Another downside to industrial agriculture is that, as we mentioned earlier, it promotes a monoculture system, where large fields of land are planted with a single type of crop. This practice is called mono-cropping. In its lacking diversity, all the normal functions of the soil are eliminated. There is no variety in insects, so there is a higher risk of plague. By not having the nutrients provided naturally by different types of plant, the soil is depleted of important microorganisms and bacteria that cannot survive in those conditions.

Together, mono-cropping, strong pesticides, and fertilizers are causing the soil in our fields to be stripped of their natural nutrients. Without nutrients, the soil cannot be fertile. Genetically modified agriculture has merely resulted in a vast production of low-quality grains, without considering the longer-term consequences.

The intensification of these agricultural practices has also caused the insect population to decrease at an alarming pace. In a 2019 study from the *Biological Conservation Journal*, the authors revealed dramatic rates of decline everywhere around the globe, which may lead to the extinction of 40% of the world's insect species over the next few decades.

Below is a chart depicting the main drivers.[27]

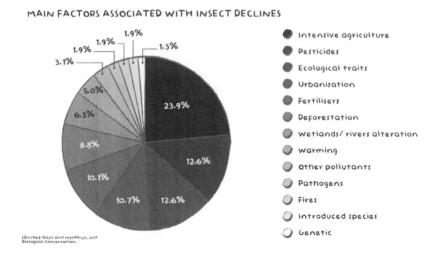

MAIN FACTORS ASSOCIATED WITH INSECT DECLINES

● Intensive agriculture
● Pesticides
● Ecological traits
● Urbanisation
● Fertilisers
● Deforestation
● Wetlands/ rivers alteration
● Warming
● Other pollutants
● Pathogens
● Fires
● Introduced species
● Genetic

Sánchez-Bayo and Wyckhuys, 2019
Biological Conservation.

In turn, since these insects are a source of food for several other vertebrates, such as fish and birds, these species are also decreasing in great numbers. As we explored previously, everything is connected. When a system starts to be unhealthily depleted, the whole chain is affected.

It is difficult to understand how this unnatural agriculture – principally, the use of Roundup – is still employed around the world today. In a 2011 article from the journal *Plant and Soil*, Monsanto's list of developed products is evaluated. This is just an extract of one of their products, Agent Orange:

> *"As a result of the use of Agent Orange, Vietnam estimates that over 400,000 people were killed or maimed, 500,000 children were born with birth defects, and up to 1 million people were disabled or suffered from health problems—not to mention the far-reaching impact it had on the health of over 3 million American troops and their offspring. Internal Monsanto memos show that Monsanto knew of the problems of dioxin contamination of Agent Orange when it sold it to the U.S. government for use in Vietnam. Despite the widespread health impact, Monsanto and Dow were allowed to appeal for and receive financial protection from the U.S. government against veterans seeking compensation for their exposure to Agent Orange.*
>
> *In 2012, a long 50 years after Agent Orange was deployed, the clean-up effort has finally begun. Yet the legacy of Agent Orange, and successive generations of body deformities, will remain in orphanages throughout Vietnam for decades to come."*[28]

I encourage you to read all this report.

The question is: how is it possible that our leaders have trusted this Biotech monster when they were already aware of its dark past? In Europe, at least, it has become more controlled. GMO-derived food must be labeled, and half of the countries which make up the European Union have opted out of a new GMO crop plan, apparently due to concerns over food safety. But in other places, like the USA for instance, the labeling of products containing some kind of GE is not even required.

Roundup is everywhere now: in our lakes, in our soil, in our children's bodies. If some governments refuse to protect their citizens, it is up to the citizens to protect themselves.

Roundup is everywhere now:
in our lakes, in our soil, in
our children's bodies. If some
governments refuse to protect
their citizens, it is up to the
citizens to protect themselves.

INDUSTRIAL ANIMAL AGRICULTURE

 A day will come in which men will look upon an animal's murder the same way they look today upon a man's murder.

– LEONARDO DA VINCI

For Steven Chu, Nobel Prize-winning physicist and former US Energy Secretary, agriculture places first for climate challenges – particularly animal agriculture.[29] Chu described the unnatural effects of industrial agriculture; what he called "oversexed corn", which devotes all its energy to making giant kernels; pigs that gain 280 pounds in a matter of months; turkeys so breast-heavy they can't mate, and must be artificially inseminated. He depicts a planet dominated by animals which have been modified, raised, and slaughtered to feed humans.

The purpose of this type of industrial farming is to maximize production whilst minimizing costs. The animals are not treated as sentient beings, but as products for consumption. The majority of them live confined in crowded, filthy conditions, receiving high doses of antibiotics to avoid illness and hormones to promote unnaturally fast growth. Often, the space is so crowded for the animals that it causes cannibalism, where the weakest or youngest are eaten by the rest. Most of them never feel sunlight or breathe fresh air; they cannot exercise, and, in fact, can barely move during their lifetime. I can easily attest that, if these factory farms were open to the public, there would be many more vegetarians.

The same awful story is repeated in most industrialized dairy farms, where the cow is separated from her newborn. This means that all the milk meant for her calf is stolen for human consumption. Soon after, the calf will most probably (and most surely, if it is male) be sent to the slaughterhouse to be sold as veal. Its mother will cry for days, longing for her baby. This same cow will be constantly artificially impregnated to repeat the cycle, and when she cannot produce any more milk (several years earlier than in a natural environment), she too will be sent to the slaughterhouse.

It is therefore easy to imagine that the chicken and egg industry (in which the chickens are usually debeaked) treats the animals which feed us with the same levels of cruelty.

This sick "agricultural" system dominates US food production today, and is growing at a fast pace in countries such as China and India. According to the Sentience Institute (an American think tank that specializes in effective altruism and social movement research), around 99% of farmed animals[30] in the US live in these unbearable conditions.[31]

What is particularly difficult to comprehend in this chain of animal suffering in the factory farm business is that it boasts not one factor that can be said to be beneficial for human health or for the planet. The con-

As animals of superior intelligence on Earth, we should feel a responsibility towards the wellbeing of other sentient beings living alongside us, instead of using and exploiting them as objects with no feelings. If we continue to eat meat, the least we can do is stop to find out where it comes from.

sumption of by-products of these tortured animals, full of antibiotics and chemicals, born and raised in packed spaces, and living in terrible conditions, will only cause our bodies to fall out of balance. Some of the health risks of consuming the food derived from these farms are antibiotic-resistant bacterial infections, food-borne diseases such as E. coli and Salmonella, and even mad cow disease. Furthermore, Viruses such as H1N1 (swine flu) or H5N1 (bird flu) evolved on chicken and pig factory farms. There is a well-established scientific link between factory farming and global pandemics.[32]

If this weren't enough, the greenhouse gas emissions caused by cattle rearing are the primary culprit of climate change. The grains and crops harvested to feed livestock are among the main reasons of deforestation. Overpopulation, alongside a high demand for meat and dairy products, are causing the destruction of our habitat at an alarming pace. This food system is so inefficient that if all the grains harvested for these animals were destined for human consumption, there would be no hunger around the world.

The way we treat our animals is a reflection of humankind. As animals of superior intelligence on Earth, we should feel a responsibility towards the wellbeing of other sentient beings living alongside us, instead of using and exploiting them as objects with no feelings. If we continue to eat meat, the least we can do is stop to find out where it comes from. Was the animal raised humanely? Did it live in a healthy environment? This is not only for the animal's sake, but for our own, too.

There is certainly no compelling reason for all these practices. Again, if we respect nature in agriculture, we could experience a positive shift in all areas. This has been put into practice with hugely successful results by Molly and John Chester: a couple from Los Angeles who decided to undertake the challenge of creating a sustainable farm. Their adventure went on to become the subject of a wonderful, award-winning documentary, *The Biggest Little Farm*; as we can see from this inspiring story, it takes time for ill and abused land to recover, but with patience and care the results can be extraordinary.

As consumers, we have the power to end this idiotic and inefficient agricultural practice, and to start pressuring the system to improve the quality of products that we buy. Good nutrition forms the foundation for good health, and eating unwell, mistreated animals is a way to become very sick. It's little wonder there are so many new diseases, mainly stemming from countries where these practices are more common.

To be able to make a change, we must start by informing ourselves of the different farming methods, and of the implications that our food choices can have on our health, on the environment, and on the welfare of animals. We must be aware of the origins of our food. We will explore this concept later on.

OVERFISHING

Tons of fish are hauled out of the sea every day at a pace that does not allow certain species to recover and replenish. Overfishing poses a major threat to our oceans, and to all wildlife that relies upon it. As fish become increasingly scarce, the survival of several coastal communities that depend upon small-scale artisanal fishing is being jeopardized. Industrialized fleets can now travel long distances to deplete fish stocks in areas where local fishermen would traditionally harvest fish in a sustainable manner.

Global consumption of marine life is outpacing natural production, causing the population of many species such as halibut, flounder, and tuna to drop dangerously low. Not only does over-fishing bring a decrease in marine life, but it also causes the death of dolphins and other large marine mammals who can become trapped in commercial fishing nets. This event is known by the term of "bycatch", causing animals to experience a horrible death by drowning or starving. Thousands of dolphins are killed every year by fishing nets, to the extent that there has been a decline of nearly 80% of dolphins in the Indian Ocean; this decline is happening every day, wherever there are commercial fishing operations.[33] We will return to discuss the idea of bycatch in later chapters.

PALM OIL AND ITS MASS DEFORESTATION

Palm oil poses another large threat to nature, as it can only be cultivated in tropical rainforests. For both its versatility and its low price, this oil is used not only in food, but also in commonly-used products such as soap, bio diesel, detergent, and shampoo. Hundreds of thousands of trees are cut down each year to produce this oil, destroying the habitat of many species – including many endangered species such as the orangutang and the Sumatran tiger. But the problem, however, does not lie in the consumption of products containing palm oil, since this is the most efficient vegetable oil to grow (as it needs less land to produce, when compared to other vegetable oils). It is possible to grow palm oil in a responsible manner, protecting nearby habitats and communities.

The organization responsible for establishing the rules for sustainable palm oil, the Roundtable on Sustainable Palm Oil (RSPO), has outlined a series of policies that many companies have adopted, frequently engaging all their supply chains, including third party suppliers and smallholders. These policies promise no deforestation, no peat development, and no exploitation (NDPE). But we still have a long way to go until all palm oil companies begin to adopt this responsible growing method.[34]

OVER-EXPLOITATION OF THE EARTH'S RESOURCES

Both the extraction of fossil fuels and the industrial agriculture practices discussed above form part of this over-exploitation of the earth. By July 29th 2019, we had already used up all the regenerative resources for the whole of that year.[35] This means that we are using more resources than the planet can regenerate in a year (Global Footprint Network). Interestingly, in 2020, due to the COVID-19 pandemic that paralyzed the world, the earth's overshoot day (which marks the day where humanity's demand for ecological resources in a given year exceeds what Earth can generate in that year) fell on August 22nd, almost one month later than the previous year. This proves that if governments take the necessary measures needed to save our planet, we can make an immediate improvement to our global footprint. If we do not act now, this date will draw closer every year. Without a change to the system, the earth's resources will run out within 30 years, and there will not be enough means to feed our ever-growing population.

It could be said that over-exploitation is inevitable, due to the escalating growth of our population, but this is a misconception. It is the desire of population to eat too much fish, too much meat, and too many animal by-products, none of which are needed for survival; this brings us, therefore, to over-exploitation. If the demand were lowered, the supply would be forced to decrease. But since the demand is continuously growing, the industrialized procedures are moving incredibly close to the realms of dangerous mass production.

POLLUTION

When we hear the word "pollution", our first thought might be air pollution. But pollution goes much further than that. Our air is not the only natural resource that is polluted – so are our rivers, streams, lakes, sea, and soil, which are all affected by human activities. This pollution is due to industrial waste such as non-biodegradable materials that end up in our water and soil. This non-biodegradable material includes feces and urine from livestock.

The quantity of plastic that ends
up in the sea continues to grow
each year, meaning a growth in
death sentences for our animals.

The excessive use of pesticides, fertilizers and GMOs, together with the burning of fossil fuels, all damage the soil, consequently reducing its fertility and causing food production to drop. At the same time, rain washes chemicals and pollutants off the fields into rivers and streams, contaminating freshwater, and poisoning the wildlife that depends on it.

Plastic pollution is one of the most alarming types of pollution. Today, there are a total of five floating garbage patches in our oceans. The first one was discovered in 1997 in the North Pacific, which now totals the size of France, Germany and Spain put together.[36] The image of the first patch discovered came to shock both the global scientific community and the general public. But this should not be a surprise, as we have been using immense quantities of plastic for several decades, and regular recycling has only recently become a habit in few select countries around the world.

Perhaps even more alarmingly, every year about 8 million tons of plastic waste end up being dumped into the oceans from coastal nations. When this plastic enters the ocean, salt water, sunlight, and wind break it down into micro particles, each the size of a grain of sand. Because of their size, these microplastics are almost impossible to be cleared from the sea.

Thousands of animals such as seabirds and fish are killed every year due to plastic and other types of garbage. Seals, sea turtles, and other mammals are killed by ingesting it or getting entangled in it. Yet the quantity of plastic that ends up in the sea continues to grow each year, meaning a growth in death sentences for our animals.

INVASIVE SPECIES

Any living organism that does not belong to an ecosystem and reproduces at a rapid pace is called an invasive species. It may not seem like a big problem, but since these species compete with native organisms for the same resources, they often have the power to do severe harm. Human activities such as global trade and transport, alongside the ever-worsening consequences of climate change, are causing ecosystems to break down, which causes an imbalance in species. In turn, when invasive species begin to overpower a habitat, native organisms may become endangered or even extinct, as they start to compete for the same food; in this instance, the invader can even outcompete native species. This might threaten the biodiversity of the ecosystem. As the earth's natural environment becomes increasingly damaged by climate change, it also becomes more vulnerable to invasive species.

This serious threat to native species and natural ecosystems is happening in our prairies, in our forests, and in our lakes and oceans. It is causing environmental harm by reducing biodiversity and leading to the extinction of some species, and major genetic changes in others. It can also directly harm the economy, when invasive organisms are accidentally introduced with crop seeds, imported plants and their soil, severely affecting crops, pastures, and land. Invasive species can also harm humans; in a recent case, the Asian tiger mosquito entered the United States in shipments of used tires from Asia. The tiger mosquito is an efficient vector for many pathogens, including dengue, West Nile virus, and encephalitis.[37]

HABITAT LOSS

All the previously mentioned causes of climate change can contribute to habitat loss or habitat destruction. This term refers to the incapacity of a damaged habitat to support its native species (plants, animals, and insects). Habitat destruction results in a loss of biodiversity and species extinction. For instance, if land is cleared for agriculture, the habitat of hundreds or thousands of species will be destroyed. Human activities such as deforestation, industrial farming, and mass urbanization all have a major negative impact upon nature. Similarly to the way this happens with humans, when an ecosystem is debilitated by pollution, deforestation, or other man-inflicted actions, it will lose its balance and will not be able to protect its living organisms, making it impossible for it to function properly or support its natural wildlife.

OVER-CONSUMPTION

 The consumption society has made us feel that happiness lies in having things, and has failed to teach us the happiness of not having things.

- ELISE BOULDING

Over-consumption is yet another factor contributing to the deterioration of the planet.

Life is much simpler than we make it. We do not need much to have our needs satisfied and enjoy a happy life. But society, mostly in the Western world, makes us believe that having more "stuff" brings more happiness. It is true that it is not easy to avoid over-consumption when living in this society; everywhere we turn, we are faced with advertisements that aim to make us believe that this or that will make us happier. We believe that this new lipstick will make us prettier, that this new car will give us admiration, or that these great toys will make our kids brighter... But the happiness that new "stuff" brings is not long-lasting. It is ephemeral, and brings only a void which grows every time we begin the vicious cycle again.

If we focus upon materialism and consume beyond our needs, nothing will satisfy our appetite for more, and the much-wanted concept of happiness will move even further out of our grasp. As we discussed earlier, happiness is about covering our basic needs, and fostering good relationships with others.

There are two other negative aspects to over-consumerism which lie hidden beneath the attractive appearance of material goods. One is the poor quality of the final product. As the price of items drop, so does quality. These goods from cheap retailers, often referred to with the term "fast fashion", are meant to last just a season, with poor-quality materials that will end up in landfills, polluting the world even further.

The other more serious consequence is that it directly feeds into modern slavery. In order to offer such low prices, these unethical companies look to source their workforce in countries where human rights are almost non-existent. To truly understand where these cheap clothes come from, and to be aware of the hard price that some must pay in order to make them, I recommend you watch the documentary *The True Cost* by Andrew Morgan. This work follows the story of Shima Akhter, a young mother who works in a fast fashion garment factory in Bangladesh. She earns less than three dollars for over ten hours of work a day. Shima decided to form a union with her colleagues, taking a list of requests to management in the hope of gaining a fairer and safter working environment. Instead, she and her fellow unionists were locked in a room by her supervisor, where several staffers proceed to beat them with sticks and chairs, so they never dared to raise their voices again.

If more people knew about the suffering and injustice that so many must endure for us to be able to enjoy this cheap clothing, we could put a stop to fast fashion and unethical manufacturing.

Over-consumption is not just a formula for a sad and empty life - it also degrades the environment. According to the UN, the fashion industry consumes more energy than the aviation and shipping industries combined.[38] Large amounts of energy are needed to create these vast quantities of unnecessary items that we buy, depleting the earth of its valuable natural resources.

The happiest individuals are not those who have the most, but those who are the most grateful for life, the kindest to others, the most optimistic in the face of difficult situations, and the most respectful towards nature and all its living beings. True happiness is much more accessible to us than we think, but most of us are not looking in the right places. Many of us are confused by the conflicting messages that society sends us. We must stop believing in misleading advertising messages solely concentrated on taking our money for superficial, short-lived goods.

02

ON KNOWLEDGE

2.1 To be a Sheep or a Thinker

 Your assumptions are your windows on the world. Scrub them off every once in a while, or the light won't come in.

— ISAAC ASIMOV

It seems that many of the problems faced by humankind in the 21st Century are rooted on biased information, or in preconceived common beliefs that don't incorporate the whole reality. By having an erroneous or incomplete view of the truth, our actions and decisions are often based on a distorted reality. Often, this illusion of knowledge can be more dangerous than a complete lack of it, for our actions based on inaccurate information may misguide us into taking wrongful actions. In more extreme cases, it could cause us to negatively and harmfully affect those around us.

There are two main reasons for this lack of clear knowledge: one has always existed and has caused many wars and conflicts around the world throughout history. It is the division that we create between us all, by creating and labeling groups according to their religion, race, economic status, or beliefs. Generally, during the lottery of birth, we automatically enter one of these groups, whether it be due to our gender, our skin color, our nationality, our parents' economic status, or their political and religious beliefs. Our parents already "belong" to "groups", so our education tends to be shaped through the characteristics of those groups. For instance, if your parents are Catholic and well-off, you might attend a private Catholic school, and coexist mainly with other Catholic families, viewing the "others" (e.g., those who are Jewish, Muslim, etc.) as different from you. In psychology, this is called "othering".

The practice of othering generally leads to a polarization of people into two groups: "us" and "them". As Polish social psychologist Henri Tajfel explains, by doing so, we tend to exaggerate the differences between groups and the similarities within our own group.[39] This approach in education often creates strong barriers and preconceived prejudices in children that are hard to eliminate in adulthood. It is a hindrance which limits life experiences and produces a deformed view of reality. This ingroup and outgroup view of the world is the root of discrimination, prejudice and racism. We are not different; we are all simply members of a big group called humanity. We all share the same desires: to be happy and to avoid pain. Seeing humankind as a whole, rather than a group of "others", encourages feelings of belonging, peace, and love for all beings.

The other reason behind the acquisition of inaccurate knowledge is more contemporary; it stems from the incontrollable burst in technology. Nowadays, we have access to an endless amount of information. Any question that we may have, any news or event that is happening around the world, is virtually instantly available to us. The problem is that this information is rarely regulated by any organization for its validity. So, often, we end up self-validating and sharing information without checking the source or truthfulness of it. We tend also to harbor a bias towards news which is already congruent with our established beliefs, further supporting the spread of erroneous knowledge.

In a 2015 report from the Media Insight Project called *How Millennials Get News: Inside the Habits of America's First Digital Generation*, more than 80% of the interviewed subjects said that at least half of their news and information came from online sources.[40] Now imagine if all this information were then shared without checking its reliability. Even Twitter was obliged to block tweets from the ex-President of the powerful USA, labeling them as misleading.

As easy as it is to get information from social networks, it is equally easy to spread it: hence the importance of fact-checking.

There is a tremendous amount of misinformation that influences us, occasionally coming even from leaders, politicians, or famous figures. Ex-President Trump, for instance, was one of the major culprits in misleading his supporters on topics such as climate change, going against the findings of scientific experts. When he was urged not to ignore science after the 2020 summer fires that ravaged California, he commented *"It'll start getting cooler, you just watch"*. In a 2020 study from Sarah Evanega et al. from Cornell University about all the false information that has been circulating around the Coronavirus pandemic, Mr. Trump appeared to be the largest driver of COVID-19 misinformation.[41] This same study evidenced the alarming consequences that misinformation might have in certain situations:

> *"In previous pandemics, such as the HIV/AIDS outbreak, misinformation and its effect on policy was estimated to have led to an additional 300,000 deaths in South Africa alone. If similar or worse outcomes are to be avoided in the present COVID-19 pandemic, greater efforts will need to be made to combat the infodemic that is already substantially polluting the wider media discourse."*

We must be more careful and selective when choosing the sources of information that will pave the way to our actions, and never share if we are not 100% sure of its validity. It is easy to manipulate ill-informed people, and the wide reach of social media has the power to control not just individuals, but society. We cannot allow all media to shape our beliefs, values, and attitudes. If we want to take an active and positive part in the history that humanity is writing at this moment, we must take control of the information that comes our way, and carefully discern what is truth from what is misinformed before acting. It is of pivotal importance that our knowledge does not only derive from what we hear or read on social platforms, but also from ourselves, our own research and findings from trustworthy sources, in order to assure the validity and reliability of the information we consume. By doing so, we can take advantage of the power of social media to inform the world of the facts about the damaging and concerning issues happening now.

2.2 The Importance of Education

 Modern man is alienated from himself, from his fellow men, and from nature. He has been transformed into a commodity, experiences his life forces as an investment which must bring him the maximum profit obtainable under existing market conditions.

FROMM 1957: 67

The world has experienced a major change over the last decade, and not just in the amount of information that we receive every day. There has also been a considerable transformation in the way we live. Technology and innovation are growing at an unbelievable speed, making life easier for some, more alienating for others, and more controlled for the rest. While it is true that this ever-growing technology allows us to stay increasingly interconnected and interdependent, it is also true that it has invoked several new challenges that society now has to face. And yet education has not been evolving in conjunction with these ever-changing challenges.

Over the course of the past century, the focus has been that of personal development, with no emphasis placed upon the greater good. It is paramount to adapt school curriculums to accommodate for subjects that will develop in accordance with the new world we are living in; subjects that aim towards the overall welfare of society, and not just personal targets.

The generations that follow will have to deal with ever-increasing challenges that we leave behind. Because of this, they will need to be as prepared as possible, in order to address them in the best way possible.

In my opinion, there are a few essential issues that must be addressed:

- Sustainable living/creativity: exploring green solutions for a cleaner, more sustainable planet.

- Health, including but not limited to nutrition, emotional balance, mindfulness, stress management, and self-knowledge (e.g., strengths and weaknesses, personal values, etc.)

- Dealing with information/critical thinking: the importance of discerning data. How to deal with mass information, selecting trustworthy sources, etc.

- Interconnection and collaboration in a global world: the history of race, and the importance of thinking globally.

- Ethics and moral values: distinction between high and low values, as we will discuss later in this book. This subject would explore not just ethics and values in society, but in technology and innovation, as well.

If we truly want to positively transform society, "Ethics and Moral Values" should not just be a new subject of study, but the philosophy of schooling itself. It has to be at the center of teaching. There are several research studies illustrating the dramatic impact of introducing human values into the school curriculum. In every case, an improvement has been detected not just in the personal development of the students, but also in the quality of their relationships and in their academic performance, resulting in a more harmonious school community. Doctor Neil Hawkes was one of the pioneers of introducing a value-based education in his school as a research study. In 1993, as the headmaster of Palmer Primary School in Kidlington, England, he developed and established over a 7-year time period an ethical program based on human values for all pupils and staff in the school. The research found the following positive outcomes:

- Underpinning the school curriculum with an education on values has a positive effect on the relationship between staff and learners, improving mental wellbeing in both.

If we truly want to positively transform society, "Ethics and Moral Values" should not just be a new subject of study, but the philosophy of schooling itself.

~~~~~~~~~~

- Value-based education encourages pupils to explore and internalize values, thereby developing a range of positive personal qualities.
- Value-based education has a greater emphasis on the development of good quality relationships between staff and parents.[42]

The world is in desperate need of ethical leadership. Education remains the most powerful tool for a better society, and yet its reforms have been based on political and commercial interests, prioritizing irrelevant skills that do not equip future generations with the essential means for tackling the many challenges that they will face. It is time to use education as a vital tool in building a better society, and to design the best possible curriculums to empower the men and women of the future.

2.3 On Values

Often, there is a sense of confusion surrounding the terms "morals" and "values". Let's begin by clarifying their meaning.

Morals are determined by the society we live in. Something that can be seen as morally acceptable within our circle could be understood to be immoral in a different environment. Homosexuality, for example, is punishable in some countries, while in others, same-sex marriage is a recognized and celebrated right.

Values, on the other hand, come from within. They are personal beliefs that dictate what is meaningful, important and right. It is our values
that guide our behavior, principles, and attitudes.

I was always of the belief that all personal values were based on
global morality and virtues. Values like honesty, humility, empathy, courage, integrity, perseverance, or discipline are highly regarded, no matter
where you are in the world. But in searching the web, I was surprised to
discover that wealth, popularity, and status all fall into the list of values.
This deeply disappointed me, as these "values" do not bring any higher

good to the person who exhibits them, or to society in general. Then again, personal values are exactly that: personal. They are not the same as virtues, for virtues are considered high in the moral standards and characteristics of an individual. When we talk about a virtuous person, it will always be in a positive manner; this does not always happen with values.

Values are what we "value" in life. The fact that values are personal means that they are relative, and not always right. Since our values form the basis of our actions, if we are interested in leaving a positive footprint upon this world, it is paramount to question the importance of our values in terms of contributing to society. There is nothing wrong with holding wealth as a value if we are planning to share this wealth to fight extreme poverty or hunger, or any other cause that will help humanity.

As an exercise, take a few minutes now to write down your top five to ten personal values. Do these relate solely to your own personal gain, or do they benefit also the welfare of humanity?

Unfortunately, in today's society, wealth is a major value and goal for many people, without the exact purpose of alleviating suffering, or making a beneficial contribution to the world.

This value, based upon financial gain, has even led to some psychologists (hopefully not many) advising parents to offer their children money in exchange for their chores. These can include things such as emptying the dishwasher or taking the dog for a walk. In fact, this was a suggestion made to me personally, when I moved to Florida with my three young children.

Today, society has become obsessed with wealth. Careers in philosophy or sociology are decreasing in popularity, merely because they don't assure high monetary benefits. In schools, subjects such as Ethics and Morality have gradually disappeared from curriculums, whereas Mathematics and Science have been prioritized. This mentality is further supported in households, where parents push their children towards careers that will secure a "bright" future: namely, one which ensures money and materialism.

Consequently, many of us do not follow the path that best fits our personality and interests. Instead, we seek the warranty of better economical revenue. In addition to lowering our values, this situation also causes a state of distress and confusion in students, where they become torn between the advice and desires of their parents and their true preferences and passions. How can we expect a moral or virtuous society if the goal of education is monetary?

The consequences are now appearing before our eyes, and can be identified in the environment, in social injustice, and in hundreds of thousands of immigrants which slip between the cracks of many cultures. By prioritizing capital, we are experiencing a crisis characterized by a lack of virtue.

True values are what form the character of an individual, as Reverend Billy Graham once stated: "*If wealth is lost nothing is lost, if health is lost something is lost; when character is lost all is lost.*" Our values are the foundation upon which we build our lives. In expressing self-centered values, we lose the drive to make a positive change in humanity.

If we want a better society, education on morality and virtues must return to school curriculums. We must teach our children by example, being kind, honest, patient, and grateful. Loving parents have the misconception that if they give their children everything they wish for, they will make them happier. But this is far from reality.

When I was a child, my mother used to keep all our toys in a locked closet. Every Friday, she would open the closet and, if we behaved well during the week, she allowed us to choose one toy to play with for the whole week. I took such great care of that special toy and would truly treasure it. Each Friday brought with it an intense excitement, just thinking of which toy I would choose next. This simple habit taught us to value our belongings; it taught us to be patient and well-behaved. One day, she decided to leave the closet unlocked for good. From then on, we were free to take any toy that we wanted at any time. Funnily enough, after a few weeks, the toys were not so precious anymore, and the happiness that we felt every Friday suddenly disappeared.

When we give too much to our children, they lose their perception of value. They want more every time. They will not learn to appreciate what they have and will not be happier. Instead, we will create insatiable and materialistic individuals that will be more focused on obtaining "things" than on meaningful experiences.

Wealth cannot buy happiness. Whilst research shows that money can increase feelings of wellbeing, it stops at a point where we have sufficient resources to cover our basic needs, and those of our family.[43] When a secure income is no longer a concern, the way we spend our earning is what influences our happiness. Spending it on somebody else brings a deeper sensation of wellbeing than using it on ourselves. This was exposed in a study published in the magazine *Science* in 2008. Elizabeth W. Dunn, Lara B. Aknin and Michael I. Norton established how prosocial spending, which means spending on others, promotes happiness and wellbeing: something which does not last when spending on oneself. The researchers conclude that *"given that people appear to overlook the benefits of prosocial spending, policy interventions that promote prosocial spending – encouraging people to invest income in others rather than in themselves – may be worthwhile in the service of translating increased national wealth into increased national happiness."*

In one of the world's longest studies on adult life and happiness from Harvard University that has lasted 75 years (and counting), scientists tracked the lives of 724 men from two groups. One group were, at that time, sophomores at Harvard College; the other group were boys from Boston's poorest neighborhoods. Every detail about their lives was recorded year after year. Dr. Robert Waldinger, the current director of this long-lasting study, concludes: *"The lessons aren't about wealth or fame or working harder and harder. The clearest message that we get from this 75-year study is this: good relationships keep us happier and healthier. Period."* He then goes on to explain that healthy social connections with friends, family and our community are good for our health and happiness, and that loneliness kills.[44]

The basis of maintaining and fostering good relationships? Being kind to others.

In conclusion, altruism and loving kindness will contribute greatly to our own wellbeing and happiness. This is something to think about when deciding our path in life.

2.4 Knowledge as a Shield

After the September 11 attacks, there was a significant rise in racism against Muslims, primarily in the US.

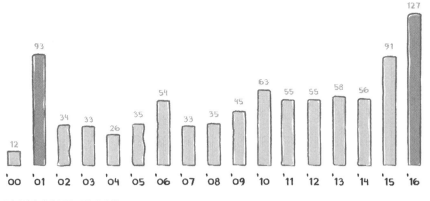

ANTI-MUSLIM ASSAULTS EXCEED 2001 TOTAL
Anti-Muslim assaults in U.S. reported to the FBI

Note: Includes simple and aggravated assaults
Source: Federal Bureau of Investigation.
PEW Research Center

According to FBI data, in 2001 there were 93 reports of anti-Muslim assaults, compared to just 12 reported in 2000.[45] Since then, the level of hate crimes towards Muslims has never returned to the relatively low statistic of 2000. This attitude was derived from a lack of understanding and knowledge of the situation which occurred. It is illogical to generalize a whole race as being guilty of the actions of one single group.

Since ex-President Trump came into office in the US, with his infamously racist rhetoric, there has been a significant rise in hate crimes across the entirety of the United States.[46] In 2018, the FBI reported that hate crimes had reached a 16-year high, with a significant increase in violence against Latinos.[47] When citizens hear their own President talk badly about other races, his political power makes it difficult for them to understand that he is not right. If bias and prejudice are instilled in individuals by their own President, this almost acts as permission to reject and even attack other groups.

The fact that information has come from our government does not necessarily make it right. We must discern the truth behind that information, rather than blindly believing it. Protecting ourselves from misleading and polarized comments is the first step in avoiding manipulation.

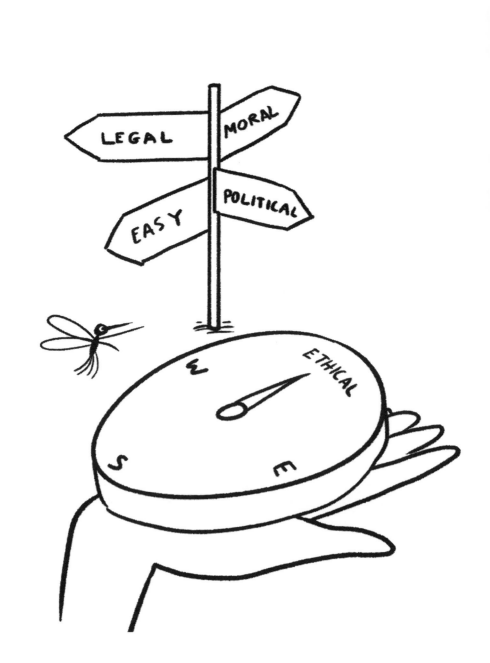

03
ON ETHICS: HUMANITY'S OTHER CHALLENGES

3.1 Self-fulfilling Prophecy

The planet is not the only thing deteriorating. I believe that, in general, human beings have lost some of their sense of kindness and caring for others. This has been shown both in the environment as well as in the social inequalities presented within it, as we discussed earlier. But it has also affected the way many fields and industries have developed. One of the reasons for this might be that the image of humanity sold to us by society is that of greed and selfishness. There are so many acts of love around us that prove this idea to be incorrect, but instead we tend to focus on the negative aspects of humanity, as exemplified by the world news.

If a person is marked by his family and friends as selfish, he will unconsciously act in accordance with this label. This is known in psychology as "self-fulfilling prophecy", a false and unfounded reality that may come true due to subconscious human responses to predictions and expectations associated with the future. It is well-documented by sociologists that labeling young adults criminals or delinquents leads to delinquent and criminal behavior.[48]

Society's negative perception towards a certain group, based on stereotypes, may encourage the group to act negatively. On the contrary, if we expect the best of the people and groups that surround us, the concept of self-fulfilling prophecy becomes a potential asset to society.

3.2 Science, Technology and Ethics

 The technologies that 50 years ago we could only dream of in science fiction novels, which we then actually created with so much faith and hope in their power to unite us and make us freer, have been co-opted into tools of surveillance, behavioral manipulation, radicalization and addiction.

– ANONYMOUS RESEARCHER, SCIENTIST AND PROFESSOR.

In this section, I will pose some questions: not with the purpose of discussing an answer, but with a view to challenging our minds on some controversial ethical issues.

In November 1998, two US scientists confirmed the successful isolation and culture of stem cells derived from human embryos and fetuses. Since then, research that involves human embryonic cells has found itself at the center of many controversial ethical debates.

Stem cells are unique cells that replicate rapidly and have the ability to become many different kinds of cells.[49] There are two types of stem cell: embryonic stem cells, derived from human embryos or fetuses, which are capable of generating into any type of human cell (pluripotent), and adult stem cells, present in most adult tissue – although these are more limited when compared to embryonic stem cells in their ability to become different cells in the body (multi-potent). Adult stem cells are used to treat and cure many types of illness, including auto-immune and cardiovascular diseases, metabolic disorders, and some types of cancers. But since embryonic stem cells are pluripotent, they can regenerate into the cells and tissues of any part of the body, thus offering a more ample spectrum of disease cures than adult stem cells.

In order to harvest stem cells from a living human embryo, the embryo must be created for this sole purpose and then destroyed. If we consider that a human embryo already displays all the characteristics required to become a unique person, that every embryo is a potential human being, is it ethical to accept the creation of embryos for the purpose of killing them afterwards? Would the potential benefits outweigh the costs? Also to be considered is the fact that, since embryonic stem cells come from another person (this being the embryo), there is a high risk that these stem cells could be rejected by the patient's body, or lead to the development of a tumor.[50] This introduces another controversial issue: the destruction of the embryo can result in the waste of a life.

In another case, the use of preimplantation genetic diagnosis (PGD), where a healthy embryo is selected among others and implanted after in-vitro fertilization, could pose an ethical dilemma for some. But let's consider this also in a different light: this process might allow the mother to avoid a later abortion if, for instance, the embryos are those of a 40+ year old woman, whose probability of carrying an unaffected embryo is very low. If, on the other hand, these embryos are chosen solely for their sex, would it be right or ethical to discard healthy embryos purely for this reason? Wouldn't this lead to a potential imbalance between sexes?

These are just some examples of the many advances that are appearing at an incredibly fast pace, and that pose an ethical dilemma in society.

Up to now, we have been able to say that the benefits of technology and science have outweighed the drawbacks, but this could easily change in the next generation. The rapid progress in biotechnology including (but not limited to) artificial intelligence, genetic engineering, cloning, and stem cell research, are escalating the debate about how far to pursue these interventions. Many of these bioethical issues raise the question of a respect for life per se. It is of vital importance to be aware of what is morally acceptable in what is technically feasible. Taking this example further, even if the research in embryonic stem cells seems promising, should the sacrifice of healthy human embryos for medical progress be allowed, if there are other viable alternatives, such as using adult stem cells which are not rejected by the patient? This would avoid the destruction of living embryos.

Although the results in embryonic stem cell research are promising, this research should adhere to moral principles more than anything else. As technology and science continue to progress, ethical boundaries must be respected when manipulating and altering natural processes in life. Society must be taken into account for decision-making and development, as well as the implementation of new technology.

3.3 Ethics on Medicine

Modern medicine: a noble and human profession or a profitable corporate business?

The 21st Century Western Medical System

There is no doubt that modern medicine has changed our lives for the better. Some of these improvements can be seen in the prevention of many diseases through vaccination campaigns, in curing infectious illnesses with the aid of antibiotics, or in treating emergencies to aid healing. There has been a dramatic global increase in life expectancy over the past two centuries.[51] Cardiovascular deaths have dropped by 40% just in the last few decades. But it is also true that 21st-Century medicine, especially within the pharmaceutical industry, has shifted its focus away from the wellbeing of the patient, and focused instead on the financial profits that can be obtained.

When a pharmaceutical company launches a new drug, the evidence of its efficiency is not always transparent, and is often based on biased and manipulated information, accentuating exaggerated benefits; studies which express negative results often go unpublished. These drug companies may even go as far as "buying" the opinion of doctors praising their product, thus making it popular among medical staff, and spending even more in publicity for promoting it than the amount they spent in research to create it. This distorted and incomplete information

Most medical staff succumb to
the commercial manipulation of
pharmaceutical organizations.

may mislead well-intentioned doctors into prescribing drugs to their patients that can cause them more harm than good.

Ben Goldacre proves this, and many other shocking and unethical practices of the medical and pharmaceutical industry, in his revealing work *Bad Pharma: How Drug Companies Mislead Doctors and Harm Patients.*[52] The author narrates several cases of specific drugs for which unpublished negative data caused much harm and even death to many patients.

Let's expose some cases which highlight a lack of transparency in the pharmaceutical industry.

In an investigation on the safety of global medical devices which lasted nearly a year, led by the International Consortium of Investigative Journalists, it was reported that across all types of medical devices *"more than 1.7 million injuries and nearly 83,000 deaths suspected of being linked to medical devices had been reported to the U.S. Food and Drug Administration over a 10-year period."* According to the investigation *"the FDA — considered by other countries to be the gold standard in medical device oversight — puts people at risk by pushing devices through an abbreviated approval process, then responds slowly when it comes to forcing companies to correct sometimes life-threatening products."*[53]

The opioid addiction epidemic in American society is yet another public health catastrophe, caused by Big Pharma. Masses of unlimited opioids were prescribed by doctors as pain relievers to patients that then became addicted. Consequently, these unethical pharmaceutical companies amassed fortunes in opioid sales - blood money gained from the suffering and pain of so many. In 2017, more than 47,000 Americans died as a result of an opioid overdose. That same year, about 1.7 million people in the United States suffered from substance use disorders related to prescription opioid painkillers. In an article by Chris McGreal, published in the *Guardian* in 2019, the manipulation of false information and consequential shameful misleading in the medical industry is evident.

"At the same time, the company (Johnson and Johnson) was working in tandem with Purdue to influence medical practice, federal regulators and politicians to promote the mass prescribing of opioids in a way no other country has seen. The two companies were competitors but also collaborators."

"They made false claims for the safety of the drugs, not least in manipulating scientific papers to promote the spurious assertion that there was a less than one percent risk of addiction from narcotic painkillers. The manufacturers funded academic studies that hewed their way and doctor training that emphasized opioids as the default treatment for pain."

Most medical staff succumb to the commercial manipulation of pharmaceutical organizations. The holistic approach in medicine is not well-regarded by most physicians, leading many patients who blindly trust pharmaceutical medicine away from trusting a natural cure. The leaders of these pharmaceutical companies have been unethically influencing the medical industry for decades, causing great pain and suffering, and gaining enormous monetary profit.

But unfortunately, healthcare systems tend to focus primarily on treating symptoms, as opposed to finding the root cause of said symptoms. In turn, patients often end up requiring a treatment that will last a lifetime, and which will likely come with accompanying undesirable side effects (whilst simultaneously filling the pockets of the practitioners). According to a survey from the National Center for Health Statistics, one of two Americans take prescription drugs. Peter C. Gøtzsche, a Danish physician, medical researcher, and leader of the Nordic Cochrane Centre at Rigshospitalet in Copenhagen, estimates that prescription drugs are the third leading cause of death globally, after heart disease and cancer.[54]

As discussed earlier, there is no doubt that what we eat plays a major role in our health. We now know that a diet based upon fruits, vegetables, pulses, and grains may reduce the risk of some forms of cancer and chronic diseases.[55] We have discovered as well that herbs and spices are full of healthy compounds that can reduce inflammation: one of the major causes of illness.[56] Yet still most physicians don't give a healthy diet the importance that it deserves. I find it difficult to believe that nutrition does not form the foundation of the curriculum for most medical training.

The good news is that integrative medicine is on the rise, which combines traditional medicine with a more holistic approach. Generally, these practitioners are a lot more compassionate towards their patients, and the treatment is often more personalized as well.

Another factor of modern medicine that has been changing negatively over the years is the impersonal "one size fits all" approach. In this method, the physician orders treatments for their patients based on incomplete personal information, and not on the specific characteristics of that particular individual. This can, in turn, cause more harm than good, as has often been the case, exemplified by the alarming frequency of medical errors. The USA is the country where this situation is most worrying, and where medical errors are one of the leading causes of death.[57] When we are unwell, we are in a vulnerable position. We need comfort, patience, and information. Patients tend to trust their doctors blindly.

Unfortunately, the relationship between patient and doctor has changed a great deal over the course of the past few decades. It has become impersonal and distanced, where the condition, and the different treatment options and their effects, are not well-explored. Medical corporations are being managed like business corporations. In the words of urologist Naeem Rahman MD.:

> *"This is more reflective of the corporatization of medicine where the principles of depersonalized mass production — highly effective in retail business models — have been imposed on health care systems, replacing the sacrosanct doctor-patient relationship with that of a commodity and consumer."*

One of the reasons for this impersonal treatment is the fact that, as discussed earlier, we are creating a sick population, causing medical staff to be overwhelmed by the volume of patients. This consequently results in a lack of time to foster a personal, compassionate relationship with their many patients. This distressed work environment causes a high level of burnout among doctors and nurses, where medical staff feel exhausted and unsatisfied with their job, leading to a mental and emotional distance from their work: the patients. According to a report from the National Academy of Medicine in the USA, as many as half of the country's doctors and nurses experience substantial symptoms of burnout, resulting in increased risk to patients, malpractice claims, worker absenteeism and turnover.[58]

Fortunately, there is hope that this impersonal means of care can change. Nowadays, the terms "personalized medicine" and "patient-centered care" are becoming increasingly trendy topics among practitioners. Medical staff have realized the importance of taking the specific characteristics of the individuals into account before making any decisions about treatment. Furthermore, patient-centered care encourages the participation of the patient and their family in every step of the decision, in order to customize a healthcare plan where patient, family, and physician feel comfortable. Let's hope that this brings a more human approach towards the patient, and that the medical industry becomes less interested in financial profits and more concerned in the wellbeing of society.

3.4 Ethics towards Animals

 The greatness of a nation and its moral progress can be judged by the way in which its animals are treated.

– MAHATMA GANDHI

This subject is one that sparked my desire to write this book: our blindness to the consequences of our actions. The fact that we are not aware of the suffering that other sentient beings endure during their short lives for just a brief moment of human enjoyment.

First, it is important to clarify that animals have feelings. There are still quite a large number of people who believe animals to be dumb, who think they solely exist for human use. Animals feel pain and suffer just as humans do. Descartes' theory of considering animals as fleshy machines without feelings has long been debunked. In the 19th Century, with Darwin's theory of evolution, we discovered that humans are just another type of animal. He argued that *"the difference between humans and other animals is one of degree rather than one of kind."*

Instead of convincing the reader of the similarities between animals and humans, I will expose instead several science-backed cases in which animals demonstrated feelings like those found in humans.

"Several years ago, a keeper at the Zoological Gardens showed me some deep and scarcely healed wounds on the nape of his own neck, inflicted on him whilst kneeling on the floor, by a fierce baboon. The little American monkey who was a warm friend of this keeper, lived in the same compartment, and was dreadfully afraid of the great baboon. Nevertheless, as soon as he saw his friend in peril, he rushed to the rescue, and by screams and bites so distracted the baboon that the man was able to escape, after... running great risk of his life." (*The Descent of Man,* Charles Darwin)

"In Kenya, researchers have watched mother elephants and other adult females help baby elephants climb up muddy banks and out of holes, find a safe path into a swamp, or break through electrified fences.

Scientists have spotted elephants assisting others that are injured, plucking out tranquilizing darts from their fellows, and spraying dust on others' wounds.

And on at least one occasion, researchers have watched an elephant struggle to help a dying friend, lifting her with her tusks and trunk, while calling out in distress." (*It's Time to Accept That Elephants, Like Us, Are Empathetic Beings,* Virginia Morell, *National Geographic,* 2014)

"It is hard to watch elephants' remarkable behavior during a family or bond group greeting ceremony, the birth of a new family member, a playful interaction, the mating of a relative, the rescue of a family member, or the arrival of a Musth male, and not imagine that they feel very strong emotions which could be best described by words such as joy, happiness, love, feelings of friendship, exuberance, amusement, pleasure, compassion, relief, and re-

spect." (*An exploration of a commonality between ourselves and elephants,* Poole 1998).

"*A dairy farmer broke down in tears as he admitted that some mother cows cry for days when their calves are taken away.*" (BBC program *The Dark Side of Dairy,* 2018)

On chimpanzees: "*Never shall I forget watching as, three days after Flo's death, Flint climbed slowly into a tall tree near the stream. He walked along one of the branches, then stopped and stood motionless, staring down at an empty nest. After about two minutes he turned away and, with the movements of an old man, climbed down, walked a few steps, then lay, wide eyes staring ahead. The nest was one which he and Flo had shared a short while before Flo died...in the presence of his big brother [Figan], [Flint] had seemed to shake off a little of his depression. But then he suddenly left the group and raced back to the place where Flo had died and there sank into ever deeper depression...Flint became increasingly lethargic, refused food and, with his immune system thus weakened, fell sick. The last time I saw him alive, he was hollow-eyed, gaunt and utterly depressed, huddled in the vegetation close to where Flo had died...the last short journey he made, pausing to rest every few feet, was to the very place where Flo's body had lain. There he stayed for several hours, sometimes staring and staring into the water. He struggled on a little further, then curled up—and never moved again*". (Goodall 1990, pp. 196–197) (Goodall J. 1990 *Through a Window.* Boston: Houghton-Mifflin)

"*Scientist Maddalena Bearzi was studying a pod of bottlenose dolphins off the coast of California. The dolphins were gathering sardines for food when, suddenly, one of them headed off in a different direction at top speed. The others followed until they were about three miles offshore and formed a circle.*

When Bearzi got there, she saw that in the center of the circle was the floating body of a teenage girl with a plastic bag wrapped around her neck. The girl had attempted suicide but was still alive. The scientists could save her because the dolphins led them to exactly the right spot having determined the girl's position through echolocation." (*Dolphins: Voices of the Ocean* by Susan Casey, Doubleday books 2015)

"A 14-year-old boy was saved from drowning by a dolphin yesterday after falling from a boat into the sea off the southeast coast of Italy, reports Philip Willan... Unable to swim, he suddenly felt himself being pushed to the surface of the water and towards his father's boat by the bottlenose dolphin, known as Filippo to local fishermen." (Dolphin saves drowning boy, The Irish Times, 2000)

"Cattle [also] can discriminate between people who handle them roughly and who are gentle with them, preferring to stand closer to those who had been gentle with them before." *"When a mother cow sees an unfamiliar vehicle approach, she will also put her body between the vehicle and her calf, presumably to protect it."* (The Psychology of Cows, Lori Marino, K. Allen, Published 2017)

"Calves are affected by the emotional pain of separation from their mother and the physical pain of dehorning. A new study finds that both types of pain can result in a negative cognitive bias similar to pessimism." (The Emotional Lives of Dairy Cows, Mary Bates, 2014)

"Abrupt and early weaning, such as occurs on the typical dairy farm, appears to be distressing for both calf and cow, says Weary," (Daniel Weary, an applied animal biologist at the University of British Columbia.) *"The calves will engage in repetitive crying and become more active,"* he says, *"and sometimes you'll see a decline in their willingness to eat solid food."* (The Emotional Lives of Dairy Cows, Mary Bates, 2014)[59]

".... This conclusion was drawn through an experiment designed to mimic chick stress. The mother hens were kept away from their chicks – they could see and hear their offspring, but they couldn't have access to them.

The baby birds were exposed to light puffs of air, which made them feel distressed, their mothers mirrored their chick's responses.

The heart rate and temperature of the birds were closely monitored, and when the chicks were distressed, the hen's heart rate and external temperature increased.

This study demonstrated that adult female birds have one of the most crucial characteristics of empathy, and that is the ability to share the emotional condition of another. "[60] (Avian maternal response to chick distress, J. L. Edgar, J. C. Lowe, S. Paul and C. J. Nicol., 2011)

"*Heart patient Jo Ann Altsman was alone when she collapsed while holi-daying in Pennsylvania. Alone, that is, except for Lulu, her pet pot-bellied pig.*

Wracked by chest pain and with no people in earshot, Jo Ann feared a new heart attack would be her last. But Lulu knew that the door flap led to a path, the path led to the road and the road led to traffic and people. So for 45 min-utes, the animal trotted between the Jo Ann and the road. When at last a man pulled over to investigate, Lulu led him straight to Jo Ann." (Hero animals: The pig that called for help, National Geographic, 2016)

If you are still in doubt, here are some scientific studies:

- "*Diana monkeys produce long-distance calls in response to predators or falling trees to alert others.*" (Zuberbühler et al., 1997)

- "*Ravens can generalize from their own perceptual experience to infer the possibility of being seen by others who are not visibly present.*"[61]

- "*A recent study from Emory University proposed that the prairie vole (a rodent found across the United States and Canada) appears to con-sole its fellow vole after scientists stress it out by giving it an electric shock.*"[62]

- "*New Caledonian crows can use tools to plan for specific future events.*"[63]

There are endless stories and scientific studies exposing the intel-ligence of animals; how they think and show feelings of distress and joy, how they care for their siblings, how they feel and act according to discernment. This can range from ravens and pigeons to lions and killer whales. We have already discussed the treatment of industrial animal agriculture, and therefore there is no need to repeat the suffering that they have to endure for the sake of human pleasure. Present-day animal agriculture, where about two in every three farm animals are raised in factory farms, goes against most of the principles we should follow in life. It is cruel, it is unethical, it is irresponsible, it is inefficient and un-healthy, and it is one of the main reasons our planet is warming up at an alarming pace. And yet we continue this process as automats, without considering the effects we are causing.

But we are now aware of the suffering that this practice brings. This

means that we have a moral responsibility to do something about it – not just for the animals' sake, but for our own. As discussed previously, younger generations are more aware than others of the sick farming industry practices currently in existence. According to an article from the *Guardian*, in the past decade, the number of vegans in the UK has risen by 350%, with this movement driven by the young; almost half of all vegans are aged between 15-34. When asked about the drive behind their decision to go vegan, the main reasons were their concern for the planet and the suffering of animals in industrial agriculture.[64]

Responsible and ethical consumers are pressuring the food system to make a radical change; vegetarians and vegans are exposing the treatment of the animals in these factory farms. They should not be alone in their fight. We need to support them to quickly in order to eradicate these buildings of torture.

DEATH AND SUFFERING OF ANIMALS AS HUMAN ENTERTAINMENT

 Truly man is the king of beasts, for his brutality exceeds them. We live by the death of others. We are burial places.

– LEONARDO DA VINCI

It would be remiss of me to leave out the suffering of animals as a consequence of human entertainment. This includes wildlife trading, circuses, bullfighting, rodeos, hunting, cock or dog fighting, animal testing, and many

more. In all these situations, the damage to animals can range from isolation, confinement, and unnatural demands to horrible suffering and death.

Let's take hunting, for instance: many hunters would say that a species like deer is "overabundant," so it is necessary to hunt them. That is a myth. The truth is that the deer population is artificially inflated by game agencies, so the hunters will always have plenty of animals to shoot.[65]

There are no surpluses in nature, and if by any chance there should be, natural processes would work to stabilize and keep a balance in all species. It is hard to believe that, currently, there are still people who use the heads of the animals they killed as decoration in their homes.

Many could argue that bullfighting is a millenary Spanish tradition, but traditions change as man and culture evolves. The purpose of this cruel source of entertainment is to kill the bull – but first the bull must suffer as the public applauds its pain and agony. This is a truly uncivilized practice, which only serves to bring more violence into the world. Many supporters of this savage means of amusement justify their interest by arguing that it is a cultural art. But art has nothing to do with torture and suffering, with violence and death, with an abuse of power over another being – all for the entertainment of the few that enjoy watching an animal be tortured and killed. It is morally unacceptable and unethical, and should be banned, along with all other sadistic practices towards animals that occur around the world.

ANIMAL TESTING

Animal testing is another practice where animal rights are violated when used as mere tools for scientific experimentation. Animals are forcefully subjected to tests that will cause them pain, permanent damage, or death. The torture, suffering, and isolation they endure is not worth the possible benefit to humans. As the biology of the animal is not the same as that of humans, many animal lives are wasted. According to The National Institutes of Health, 95 of every 100 drugs that pass animal tests *fail* in humans. Furthermore, up to half of animal experiments are worthless, and are never even published. In this technological era we are currently living through, there are other means of testing the toxicity of products which, most of the time, are more effective than animal testing. This testing methodology places humans at its center, including organs-on-chips, organoids, human-based micro-dosing, in vitro technology where human cells and tissues are used, human-patient simulators, and sophisticated computer modeling; these are all cheaper, faster, and more accurate than animal tests.[66] In June 2013, Elias Zerhouni, former Director of the National Institutes of Health (NIH), made this comment in an animal research fund meeting:

"We have moved away from studying human disease in humans... We all drank the Kool-Aid on that one, me included... The problem is that [animal testing] hasn't worked, and it's time we stopped dancing around the problem... We need to refocus and adapt new methodologies for use in humans to understand disease biology in humans." —Doctor Elias Zerhouni

We have the privilege of being the most powerful living beings on the planet, and as such, we have a moral obligation to take care of all other forms of life around us. We ought to treat animals with dignity and respect. After all: we are animals, too. It is truly sad to witness how humanity unknowingly exploits this privilege and takes advantage of that power, inflicting suffering and death onto all forms of life simply for selfish human gain.

Hopefully, a few decades from now, all these abusive and cruel practices towards animals will be seen as a moral atrocity. Animals are not 'property', and do not exist for our use and pleasure. Let's begin to see them for what they are: SENTIENT beings that can grieve and suffer just as we do.

IF FISH COULD CRY

Evidence is now accumulating that commercial fishing inflicts an unimaginable amount of pain and suffering. We need to learn how to capture and kill wild fish humanely – or, if that is not possible, to find less cruel and more sustainable alternatives to eating them.

– PETER SINGER

The suffering of ocean life caused by humans is often neglected. The practice of catching millions of fish and letting them die slowly by suffocation is barbaric. But there are no slaughter requirements or legal protection for fish, despite several studies confirming that fish feel pain.[67] According to the Consortium for Wildlife, at least 7.3 million tons of marine animals are accidentally caught every year. It is not uncommon for bycatch to exceed the targeted catch. Among the incidental catch are not just other fish species but also sea turtles, dolphins, porpoises, seals, or sea birds. In fact, bycatch is one of the biggest global threats to dolphins and whales. The animals caught accidentally are just returned to the ocean, either dead or left to die an agonizing death.

Stricter regulations are gradually coming into place in some countries (unfortunately not in ALL countries), but there is still a lot more to be done. ALL countries should impose severe regulations and, most importantly, authorities should make sure they are followed. Despite new fishing gear and technology to avoid or lessen the issue, such as gillnets containing barium sulphate to make them more visible, or special nets with openings for turtles, too few people are using this equipment, and bycatch is sadly increasing in intensity and frequency. More control and regulation in fishing activities is needed, as well as a greater investment in fishing technology to decrease the staggering amount of wasted sea life. This, in turn, could remedy the threat to many species.

3.5 Ethics and Altruism

"On your way to work, you pass a small pond. On hot days, children sometimes play in the pond, which is only about knee-deep. The weather's cool today, though, and the hour is early, so you are surprised to see a child splashing about in the pond.

As you get closer, you see that it is a very young child, just a toddler, who is flailing about, unable to stay upright or walk out of the pond. You look for the parents or babysitter, but there is no one else around. The child is unable to keep her head above the water for more than a few seconds at a time. If you don't wade in and pull her out, she seems likely to drown. Wading in is easy and safe, but you will ruin the new shoes you bought only a few days ago and get your suit wet and muddy. By the time you hand the child over to someone responsible for her, and change your clothes, you'll be late for work. What should you do?"

The drowning child is a hypothetical case used by esteemed Australian philosopher Peter Singer in his book *The Life you can Save* to expose our moral responsibility to save lives, especially if doing so doesn't pose any danger to yourself, or a loss of something of comparable moral value.[68] The answer to this question is obviously predictable. Singer then argues that there is no moral difference between a child drowning before your eyes and the millions of children "drowning" every day in preventable diseases or extreme poverty. According to the international relief agency Mercy Corps, around 9 million people die of hunger every year (whilst, ironically, the USA wastes 30% to 40% of its food supply); every two minutes, a child dies of malaria.[6970] Yet we all have the power to end all this pain.

There is a lot of suffering due to extreme poverty around the world that could be easily avoided. Not everyone is lucky enough to be born into a safe and economically-secure environment, or with the same opportunities provided to many others. It can also be said that extreme poverty is indirectly caused by affluent nations. Developed countries have been damaging the environment for decades, and, as we discussed earlier, the consequences are mostly felt in poor countries. Droughts, heat waves, and flooding have had a dramatic effect upon agriculture: one of the main activities in these countries. This is yet another reason why we have an

obligation to contribute to the eradication of extreme poverty; it is a question of fairness, especially as it does not require a big sacrifice from our part to save lives.

As Singer puts it: "*a modest contribution from everyone who has enough to live comfortably would suffice to achieve the goal of lifting most of the world's extremely poor people above the poverty line of $1.90 per day. If that modest contribution were given, we would no longer be in the situation in which children go blind due to vitamin A deficiency or get malaria because they don't have anti-malarial medication or bed nets or die from diarrhoea when they could have been saved by treatments costing pennies.*"

Often, we have a will to help, but we can find ourselves getting lost within the vast number of charities, not knowing which will help us do the most good. We may also wonder if our donation would go towards something such as administration fees, as opposed to going directly to the cause.

Nowadays, there are non-profit organizations such as GiveWell who are dedicated to the search for NGOs which truly make the most difference, and where transparency and effectiveness are at the center of the charity.

So, if it requires so little to save lives, but makes an enormously positive difference among the most vulnerable people on Earth, there should be no doubt when making the decision to donate. We would not only help to alleviate suffering, but would also help ourselves, as altruism has proven to bring happiness, and better health and wellbeing, among many other benefits.

3.6 Environmental Ethics

As discussed in previous chapters, we are living in the Anthropocene Era: a time when human beings are using all resources on the planet at a pace at which the earth does not have time to regenerate those resources. We are neither respecting nor thinking about other forms of life on the planet, or the generations to come. Pollution and depletion caused by industrialized countries are not considering developing countries, which, as we saw earlier, are those most affected by climate change; global capitalism has already imposed detrimental consequences onto nature. But the proposed "technological fixes" are even more worrying; instead of addressing the root causes, they suggest large-scale interventions in nature that, according to experts, may cause even further damage by inducing novel changes in climate.[71]

Geo-engineering is a term used to describe different strategies which deliberately manipulate the climate to reduce the warming of the earth. One of these techniques, in the field of solar geoengineering, is to inject sulphate aerosols into the stratosphere to block out sunlight. Despite the risks and dangers that geo-engineering poses to humanity, this field is attracting large quantities of investment and research funds.[72]

Such "fixes" pose also another ethical issue. This geo-engineering research is funded mainly by a small, elite group of billionaires who, if we continue to support them, will have the power to manipulate the earth's climate. This in itself poses a risk since, until now, we have witnessed many cases of social injustice caused by the powerful towards the rest of humanity.

The solution to climate change is obvious, and we are all aware of it. We simply need to leave most fossil fuels in the earth, shifting from extraction to renewal. We must stop exploiting a planet that we share with countless other beings, and understand that, in order for us to survive, we have to respect all life around us.

Climate change does not just affect nature, but also poses social, political, and economical repercussions, bringing new forms of inequality and injustice. Instead of funding projects that will continue to damage the environment, finances should be directed towards ethical solutions based on global justice and a respect for nature.

Climate change does not just affect nature, but also poses social, political, and economical repercussions, bringing new forms of inequality and injustice.

04
ON YOURSELF

4.1 The Difficult Task of Discovering Yourself

 Knowing yourself is the beginning
of all wisdom.

—ARISTOTLE

Many factors influence our view of the world. As discussed previously, every individual has a different reality created by their
own thoughts, past experiences, and perceptions. It is as if we
all see the world through a filtered lens, made just for us. Ekhart Tolle, the
renowned German spiritual teacher and bestselling author, insists that
*"your perception of the world is a reflection of your state of consciousness. [...]
Every moment your consciousness creates the world you inhabit."* This is not
a problem in itself. But the problem arises when we are convinced that
our personal reality is identical to that of everyone else.

To understand what the world is truly like, we need to adopt a vision
that is as objective as possible. We must first understand why we think
the way we do, why we see reality the way we see it. We must stop and
travel into our deepest consciousness to discover ourselves, for this is
the first step in becoming self-aware. By really knowing ourselves, we
can understand why we do the things we do, as this is paramount to
becoming conscious of our own actions and understanding their conse-

quences. This is essential for making decisions in accordance with our own values. So, if we want to really make a difference, let's take a journey into our soul.

The Pain of Unrealistic Comparison

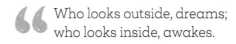 Who looks outside, dreams;
who looks inside, awakes.

— CARL JUNG

The way society behaves has changed greatly in recent decades. The enjoyment of life's experiences is increasingly being influenced by a small screen. We are so concerned with sharing our happy moments on social networks that we forget to fully appreciate them. Now more than ever, with the ever-growing presence of social media, we are constantly comparing ourselves to others. But we must remember that this is not a realistic comparison. These networks reflect an untruthful society, where images are filtered and carefully chosen to reflect the 'highs' and mask the 'lows' of peoples' lives. The images shared are not the whole reality. Failures, sadness, and imperfections, which are inevitable to us all, don't make it onto our profiles. As a result of seeing others' rose-tinted lifestyles, constant comparison is unavoidable, often leading to envy, loneliness, or even depression – no matter how much we have in life.

Psychologist Melissa Hunt from the University of Pennsylvania knows this very well. In 2018, she led a study on the relationship between social media and depression.[73] 143 participants were divided in two groups; in one group, the time spent on Facebook, Instagram and Snapchat was limited to 10 minutes a day per platform, while the other control group could use it as much as they liked. After three weeks, the participants who spent limited time on social media reported feeling less sad and lonely than the group used social networks with no time limit. *"Using fewer social media than you normally would leads to significant decreases in both depression and loneliness. These effects are particu-*

larly pronounced for folks who were more depressed when they came into the study," concludes Hunt.

Another interesting fact about the use of these networks is how the hormones dopamine, "the pleasure chemical", and oxytocin, the "cuddle chemical", are released every time we receive a "like" or a positive comment in our posts.[74] The neurotransmitter dopamine is released into our body when we have a pleasant experience (e.g., eating something that we love, or having successful social interactions). Oxytocin, on the other hand, is stimulated when we show affection or love. Because these chemicals play a major role in our happiness, our brain uses them to motivate us to repeat the action that caused us pleasure. But the role these hormones play when it comes to social media can very often lead to addiction.

 You can search throughout the entire universe for someone who is more deserving of your love and affection than you are yourself, and that person is not to be found anywhere. You, yourself, as much as anybody in the entire universe, deserve your love and affection.

– BUDDHA

There is no perfect life. In comparing our world to that of a filtered illusion, we are wasting opportunities to appreciate valuable moments and pockets of happiness that may never return.

Don't get me wrong: these social networks have many benefits for their users. As somebody who has lived most of her life away from family and friends, I can say that the use of social media can be a lifesaver in allowing you to feel closer to your loved ones. The problem is the way we are using it, and the time that we are dedicating to it. As with everything, balance is key. An abuse of social media might prove a hindrance to our self-knowledge and life fulfilment, in that the importance we are attributing to others' lives might steal valuable time from our own intro-spection.

If you notice that social networks are beginning to emotionally affect you, make a conscious effort to only follow people who inspire you, who make you feel good, and who help you become a better you, instead of those who bring you down. Limit your time on such platforms – you will find yourself with a great deal of extra time that you can use more proac-tively. You will feel lighter and happier. I can assure you that you will not miss it, even for a moment.

Every Cloud has a Silver Lining

It took me several decades to realize that I was living my life for oth-ers. I would do what was expected of me; I would live as others wanted me to live. I was extremely influenced by my environment, my friends, my family. This molded me into a person that was not my true self, but rather an accumulation of traits modeled on pleasing the people around me. Before I knew it, my essence was disappearing, leaving in its place a jumbled 'copy' of others. This quickly led to low self-esteem and a perma-nent sense of dissatisfaction with my life.

But this situation changed when misfortune hit my family. I was forced to put a sudden stop to my mundane life. My new situation led me to isolate myself from others and forget about social networks. My stress and anxiety were so severe that I developed an acute facial eczema that negatively affected my everyday life. In a desperate attempt to con-trol it, I began to meditate, trying to be more mindful about small things in life. This sudden transformation in my lifestyle brought me a new sense of reality. By gifting myself with more time alone, gradually, I be-gan to change and discover who I really was. By gaining more profound self-knowledge, I felt released from the need to follow the steps of oth-ers. I felt a liberation from the pressures of society, and at the same time, more self-confident than I had ever felt before. I was finally at peace with myself.

After this powerful personal experience, I have come to realize that, often, the most meaningful lessons in life are learned through the most difficult times. Calamities are wake-up calls to help you see reality more clearly. Although this is not the case for everyone, those who live a life without adversities may continue to find their reality empty of true meaning, following a path marked by others, and completely ignorant of their own purpose in life.

Even if we don't realize it, without self-knowledge, the decisions that we make are influenced by the society we live in; this, in turn, takes us further away from our true self. We might think that we know our "self", but many times it is a reflected "self", fabricated by what others say about us. When this happens, we may lose our ability to think by ourselves, causing us to enter into an irrational herd mentality.

Knowledge and acceptance of oneself are the starting point for every venture, no matter how big or small. It is the first step to take if we want to thrive in whatever we do. But it is not an easy task. For most of us, our inner self could be like a strict parent who is always criticizing our actions, reactions, attitudes, and decisions. For this reason, we tend to think the people around us are better than us, compelling us to follow in their footsteps. But this is the worst thing we can do. Instead, we must accept and be happy with ourselves and the life that we have, enjoying the ups and learning from the downs. We are truly unique in this world; no two people are the same. Let's embrace this uniqueness.

Since this is no easy task, we will need some tools and allies in order to persevere.

4.2 Self-Interrogation for Self-Knowledge

Perhaps a few sessions of self-interrogation are a good place to start on the path to self-discovery. If we think about the great importance of the actions and decisions that we make in our lives, it may seem difficult to believe that this self-interrogation practice is not a common activity for most of us. Consequently, the motive behind our actions may not lie in accordance with our true selves. Take a few minutes to ask yourself these questions:

- Am I living as fully as I should be?
- Am I happy being me?
- Do I envy others?
- Do I persistently compare myself to others?
- Do I know my values in life?
- Do I truly understand my strengths and weaknesses?
- Do others' opinions mold my own thoughts?

Self-questioning is important for self-knowledge. Comparison and envy are clear signs of a lack of acceptance of the self, inasmuch as a discovered self prevents unrealistic comparison. By valuing the opinions of others over our own, we are reinforcing a sense of low self-esteem. Of course, it is important to listen to other people's opinions, taking them into consideration in order to develop our own perspective. Yet we must not abandon our own thoughts merely to embrace the points of view of others. In order to assess our personal growth, the comparisons we make must be with our own past self, for this is the only path for self-growth.

Hidden Strengths and Highlighted Weaknesses

 Compassion for others begins with kindness to ourselves.

— PEMA CHODRON

When working on the discovery of oneself, it is of vital importance to have an objective understanding of our own strengths and weaknesses.

The level of self-esteem that we possess largely depends on the way in which we were raised as children. There are parents who are aware of the importance of respecting the individuality of each child, and others that have a standard idea of what a perfect child must be, as if they were products in a factory, all produced by the same universal mold – void of uniqueness. Nonetheless, if we are permanently criticized from a young age, it is hard for us to accept the way we are. We learn to highlight our weaknesses and hide our strengths. It is very difficult to overcome a history of unacceptance determined by our past. But the truth is that we are what we think. The exterior world sees us as we see ourselves; if we only focus on our flaws, our abilities and strengths will disappear from view, both for ourselves and others. Yet, if we do the exact opposite, honing our attention in on our strengths and learning from our mistakes, our weaknesses will not be so defined, and we will discover a new potential that we did not even know we had.

Self-compassion is of vital importance to overcoming any obstacles from our past that might define us. By developing self-compassion, we relieve ourselves of our own suffering. Without it, we will not be able to grow spiritually or feel compassion for others. We have to start with ourselves.

4.3 Toolkit for Self-Acceptance: Mindful, Thankful and Optimistic Minds

Mindfulness for a Peaceful Outlook

We usually live our lives and our routines in an almost robotic way, without taking time to appreciate our surroundings or notice our subtler feelings. Mindfulness means being fully aware of the present moment, deeply conscious of what our five senses are experiencing. It means being fully engaged in whatever activity we are doing, without judgement. There have been several studies which have proven the benefits of mindfulness. In one study led by I. Schreiner and J. Malcolm in 2012, 50 participants who suffered from depression, anxiety and/or stress were asked to take part in a ten-week mindfulness meditation program. At the end of the program, the severity levels of all affective measures had decreased in all participants; those who had a severe form of emotional difficulty before the start of the study were those who demonstrated a higher improvement over time.[75]

The benefits of mindfulness are not limited to reducing stress, anxiety, and depression; they go much further. Mindfulness enhances memory and concentration, improves the quality of our sleep, reduces high blood pressure, and more. As with all worthwhile things in life, practice makes perfect. Initially, the process will be difficult. You may struggle to focus on the present moment for a long time. Don't be disappointed or give up, as success will come for those who continue trying. Even if at the beginning you can only control your wandering mind for 5 to 10 minutes at a time – for instance, in feeling the sun on your skin, or hearing and appreciating the sound of the birds – that is an achievement in itself. You will notice how, eventually, your time spent in mindful bliss will increase as you continue your practice.

By living a more mindful life, and as we appreciate the small details of happiness that previously went unseen, we will spontaneously become more grateful and optimistic.

Gratitude and Optimism for a Happy Mind

It is so difficult to be grateful in a fast-paced, materialistic society. How often do we live our lives without even realizing how fortunate we are to have a job, family, friends, health, and so many other gifts that we usually take for granted?

We tend to center our attention on what we are missing. It is only when we lose something valuable to us, like our health or a loved one, that we realize just how much we have.

For some, gratitude comes more naturally than others, whether this is due to nature, nurture, or even a combination of both. The fact is that if gratitude is not something that we practice, it would be beneficial for us to train ourselves to adapt this habit into our lives. Every day, we can dedicate a few minutes a day to thinking about all the things that we should be grateful for, even writing these thoughts down in a journal. Although gratitude may seem a simplistic emotion, it is a powerful one.

Psychologists Robert Emmons from the University of California and Michael McCullough from the University of Miami led a study for ten

By living a more mindful life, and as we appreciate the small details of happiness that previously went unseen, we will spontaneously become more grateful and optimistic.

weeks to show how powerful gratitude can be. They randomly assigned participants to three different groups: the first group had to briefly write down in a journal five things that they were thankful for. The second group had to do exactly the opposite: they were encouraged to write down things that happened that made them upset or irritable. The neutral control group just had to describe five events that had affected them in a positive or negative way. At the end of the ten weeks, participants of the group that kept a gratitude journal felt happier and more optimistic than the rest of the participants, and also reported feeling fewer symptoms of physical illness.[76]

It takes just five minutes a day to develop our gratitude, and the benefits are so worthwhile.

4.4 A Word on Meditation

 To understand the immeasurable, the mind must be extraordinarily quiet, still.

– JIDDU KRISHNAMURTI

Meditation has been practiced for thousands of years, but its benefits have only been recognized recently in the Western world.

Meditation is very similar to mindfulness: the difference is that meditation is a formal, seated practice with a time limit, whilst mindfulness refers to the act of being present in every task we carry out in our day-to-day lives. Both practices help us to calm the mind and exist fully in the present moment. The purpose is to achieve a clearer and more stable mind; in fact, the nature of the mind is already clear and calm, but the noise of the outside world, with its mundane pleasures and activities, makes us confused and unstable.

There have been countless studies linking the benefits of meditation to our general wellbeing. This practice can actually modify the brain's structure and function. Richard Davidson – prominent neuroscientist and expert in emotions and the brain – has carried out extensive research in the effects of meditation on the brain. In his 2017 book *Altered Traits: Science Reveals How Meditation Changes Your Mind, Brain, and Body*, Davidson and science journalist Daniel Goleman expose the many benefits of a daily meditation practice.[77] Among other effects, daily meditation can:

- Increase our empathy and compassion towards others,

- Moderate our emotions,

- Reduce stress reactivity,

- Enhance our concentration and focus,

- Help reduce suffering.

Furthermore, they discovered that meditation can be equally effective as medication for treating anxiety, depression, and pain – but without the side effects.

Many studies like this have proven that meditation can improve our general wellbeing, even bringing us closer to happiness.[78] The benefits are endless; but still, many of us don't understand the point in calming the mind. In order to progress in this transformative practice, it is important to understand WHY we meditate, before learning HOW to meditate.

Most of us dedicate a good part of our daily routine to taking care of our body: we work out, we eat healthily. We also have a strong focus upon developing our profession, and upon learning new skills to be able to make a good living. But we generally tend to neglect our mental health, keeping ourselves permanently busy – not just on a surface level, but in our minds as well, masquerading silence with any kind of noise. This may not be a great strategy, as no matter how much we do for our body, without a stable mind, the results are limited.

Anxiety and depression are just some of the ailments caused by an unstable mind. The mind is the most important part of any human being. Our thoughts stem from our mind, and based on these thoughts, we perceive and interpret reality. Our mind is the most powerful tool we possess to be able to do good for ourselves and for others; but if uncontrolled, it can also be a destructive force in our life. By controlling our thoughts, we are deciding how to live. One of the best ways to take care of your mind is by dedicating some of your daily routine to the practice of meditation.

In my case, it was not easy to start practicing meditation. I have always had a very wandering mind. At the beginning, I felt I was just wasting my time, sitting and not doing anything. Luckily, at that time, I was in close contact with a friend who practiced meditation, and who therefore helped me avoid common mistakes and improve my practice; we will discuss this later, but one of these common mistakes is to harbor patience. When we don't see immediate results, we might feel we are not progressing, and therefore might abandon the practice. But even if you don't feel like it, you are progressing. Patience and perseverance are key factors. For some there is a breakthrough point, where the effort and consistency start to pay back; for others it comes gradually. For everyone, it transforms lives.

There are several ways to meditate, but if you are just starting out with your practice, the main goal is to silence the mind. Do not concentrate on your thoughts; acknowledge them, but let them pass by, just be. This can be achieved through music or chants, reciting a mantra, concentrating our mind on an object and visualizing it, or just being silent and focusing on your breath. It is recommended that you start gradually, with maybe five to ten minutes every morning and/or night for a week or two, and then extending the meditation to five more minutes every few weeks. It is very important to practice every day, even just for a few minutes. If you do this, you will start to feel the results relatively quickly.

Here are some mistakes to avoid:

- Don't stop your practice, not even for a day. Even if just for five minutes, make sure to meditate every day.

- Before starting your meditation practice, find a comfortable position. It does not matter whether this is sitting on a chair or on the floor, but you must be comfortable to avoid any movement during the session. This way, you will not be distracted if you start to feel uncomfortable.

- Try not to meditate with external aids. Although for beginners this can be a good way to start, the point of meditation is to encounter your deepest self. When you meditate using an app, music, or guided meditation, you are losing the chance to experience personal insight in your meditation

- Don't expect immediate results. This is a practice that will positively transform your life in every aspect, so give it time and patience. I can assure you that if you do, you will be on your way to a better and wiser self.

The ways to meditate are as endless as the benefits of meditation. You must find the technique that best suits your personality or your lifestyle. I can assure you that engaging in this adventure will change your life forever, in the most positive way you can imagine.

4.5 The Discovery of Compassion.

 Compassion is the basis of morality.

- ARTHUR SCHOPENHAUER

Compassion is the noblest and most powerful of all qualities. If we all had to choose just one value that take us further in doing good, for oneself as well as for others, that value would be compassion. It encompasses many other virtues within it: kindness, empathy, courage, acceptance, and generosity.

Compassion can sometimes be confused with empathy, but there is a vital difference between them. Empathy causes one to be moved by the suffering of others but does not necessarily entail doing anything to alleviate their pain. Although it is a good place to start in the search for a

One day, a man was walking along the beach when he noticed a boy picking something up and gently throwing it into the ocean. Approaching the boy, he asked, "What are you doing?" The youth replied, "Throwing starfish back into the ocean. The surf is up and the tide is going out. If I don't throw them back, they'll die." "Son," the man said, "don't you realize there are miles and miles of beach and hundreds of starfish? You can't make a difference!"

After listening politely, the boy bent down, picked up another starfish, and threw it back into the surf. Then, smiling at the man, he said: "I made a difference for that one."

- LAUREN EISLEY

better self, it will not take you very far, and does not do anything to make this world a better place to live. It is a feeling with no engine. Compassion, on the other hand, makes us want to *do* what we can to alleviate the suffering of others. It is a feeling that takes us far. Empathy founded is within compassion. Charities are founded by compassionate people, in the way that the lives of people in war zones are saved by compassionate doctors.

Contrary to previous beliefs about human nature, there is a growing body of research suggesting that we are born wired for goodness. In the book *The Compassionate Instinct* by psychologist Dacher Keltner of UC Berkeley, leading scientists and science writers present a series of empirical research and personal stories about new science on human kindness.[79] This is an excerpt from the findings:

> "University of Wisconsin *psychologist Jack Nitschke found in an experiment that when mothers looked at pictures of their babies, they not only reported feeling more compassionate love than when they saw other babies; they also demonstrated unique activity in a region of their brains associated with the positive emotions. Nitschke's finding suggests that this region of the brain is attuned to the first objects of our compassion—our offspring.*
>
> *But this compassionate instinct isn't limited to parents' brains. In a different set of studies, Joshua Greene and Jonathan Cohen of Princeton University found that when subjects contemplated harm being done to others, a similar network of regions in their brains lit up. Our children and victims of violence—two very different subjects, yet united by the similar neurological reactions they provoke. This consistency strongly suggests that compassion isn't simply a fickle or irrational emotion, but rather an innate human response embedded into the folds of our brains."*

If compassion is an innate emotion embedded in human nature, how can there be so much suffering caused by human beings? There are so many factors that intervene in the behavior of every individual: factors that will dictate our reaction when confronted with the suffering of other sentient beings. For those raised surrounded by kindness and openness towards all others, it is easier to develop a compassionate heart;

but for those who have experienced a rougher start in life, feelings of empathy and benevolence towards others would be harder to develop.

Even so, we all have the potential to develop compassionate feelings. By developing a practice of self-knowledge, mindfulness, and gratitude, all based in self-compassion, true compassion will follow. With training, constancy, and patience, the veils accumulated over time can be pushed aside to allow our natural compassion to flourish.

In another article by Keltner, *The Compassionate Species*, he goes on to state that: *"We became the super caregiving species, to the point where acts of care improve our physical health and lengthen our lives. We are born to be good to each other."*

We have discussed previously how good relationships and altruism foster a better quality of life and feelings of wellbeing. In this way, compassion also brings benefits to our own general health. Ed Diener and Martin Seligman, leading researchers in positive psychology, suggest that when we connect with others in a meaningful way, it helps us enjoy better mental and physical health, and speed up recovery from disease.[80] Further research on the subject performed by Sara Konrath at the University of Michigan and Stephanie Brown at Stony Brook University, shows that it may even make us live longer. [81]

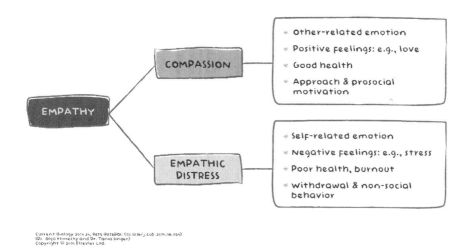

Current Biology 2014, R875-R878 DOI: (10.1016/j.cub.2014.06.054)
(Dr. Olga Klimecky and Dr. Tania Singer)
Copyright © 2014 Elsevier Ltd.

Compassion and empathic distress. Schematic model that differentiates between two empathic reactions to the suffering of others.[82]

Many times, when we are over-exposed to the suffering of others, this might lead to distress and negative feelings. This carries with it the danger of emotional burnout. There is a kind of meditation in loving-kindness, inspired in the Eastern contemplative tradition, which is very powerful, and helps to regulate our negative feelings when exposed to the suffering of others. In a study by Olga Klimecki, a researcher at the Max Planck Institute for Human Cognitive and Brain Sciences in Germany, participants were shown videos of people in distress (e.g., crying after their home was flooded) before and after receiving a one-day loving-kindness meditation class. In this class, they practiced extending feelings of warmth and care toward themselves, a close person, a neutral person, a person in difficulty, and complete strangers, as a way of developing their compassion skills. They found that the compassion training led participants to experience significantly more positive emotion when viewing the distressing videos. In other words, they seemed better able to cope with distress and negative feelings than they did before the training—and they coped better than a control group that did not receive the compassion training.

By practicing loving-kindness meditation, Negative feelings like anger, sadness, or stress will be slowly replaced by other positive emotions like joy, happiness, and love.[83]

It is not difficult to feel compassion towards people that we like; the real challenge is to reach a point where we can feel loving kindness towards our enemies. Once we have achieved this, we will understand that their actions and their malice are often derived from ignorance and confusion, and that those acts don't represent them. When we can honestly wish them happiness, and hope for an end to their suffering, we will have achieved the most difficult and most valuable kind of compassion.

At this moment in history, where humanity's general viewpoint is individualistic, we urgently need more love and compassion towards all forms of life. According to new research, "people who believe in oneness – the idea that everything in the world is connected and interdependent – appear to have greater life satisfaction than those who don't, regardless of whether they belong to a religion or don't."[84]

We need to feel a connection among us all. A centered and selfish way of thinking only brings more pain and isolation. When we stop thinking about our own suffering and open our minds and hearts with compassion to the suffering of others, our pain becomes more bearable, as our focus is no longer on ourselves, but on the other. Simply understanding that we all face the same problems and suffering in life, and that we all want to be happy, allows us to overcome isolation and feel the interconnection that exists among all living things on Earth. I am a firm believer that, just by changing our behavior to be kinder and more loving towards all living beings, we will attract not only a happier future, but also more loving and caring people.

Like the boy in the starfish story, we cannot solve all the suffering in the world. But with a compassionate heart, we can do a lot to alleviate the pain of those within our reach.

05
YOU CAN MAKE
A DIFFERENCE

We ourselves feel that what we are
doing is just a drop in the ocean. But
the ocean would be less because of that
missing drop.

– MOTHER TERESA

This is where you come in. We have the power to make a change together. We cannot wait for our leaders to do something; now, there is a sense of urgency for change. It is no longer an option. Curious to find out what you can do?

5.1 In Agriculture

- Support Local, Sustainable Farmers

  It is difficult to come to terms with the fact that, by choosing to purchase cheap meat, we are promoting factory farming: a process that causes an incredible amount of animal suffering. We are negatively affecting local farmers that still care about ethical agriculture and animal welfare; we are playing a part in the destruction of our ecosystem. And, if this weren't enough, we are damaging our health, too. However, by supporting local farmers, these negative consequences can be reversed. In this way, we can become a vital part of the change needed to achieve a sustainable food system, where the animals, the earth, and our bodies will be respected.

It is important to note, however, that in some cases, buying locally is not always the best choice in lessening our footprint. It is wiser to buy produce from areas where it is grown naturally due to the climate and soil, such as the oranges in Florida, USA or Valencia, Spain. Since these oranges are grown naturally in these areas, buying them leaves a lower footprint than local oranges in areas where they do not grow naturally, due to the artificial production processes involved.

- Find Out the Origin of your Food

  It won't always be possible to buy from local farms, but there are several other ways to support a responsible, ethical, and compassionate food system.

  In some countries, it is now possible to find out more about the animals we consume. Product labels can tell us if the animal was raised humanely, or if the dairy produce was collected in an ethical manner that cares for the cows, sheep, or goats. Of course, because these ethical farmers run through more expenses than the factory farms to guarantee fair animal treatment, their products tend to be more expensive. Nonetheless, it is a beneficial choice as much for our own health as for the planet.

- When buying products containing palm oil, check carefully that is has been made with certified sustainable palm oil.

- Buy organic when possible.

  Buying organic produce will always be more expensive than regular produce, just because it costs significantly more to grow, process, and ship small quantities of organic food. However, it is indubitably better for our health, and for the planet. If we create a higher demand for such products, little by little, the price will decrease, and we will help to raise the quality of our food system.

  If your budget is restricted, a good option is always to buy your food in a local farmers' market, even if this produce is not organic. It would be wise also to lower your consumption of animal produce. By eating animal by-products around two or three times a month, but ensuring that it is of the best quality, you would decrease both your expenses and your footprint, as well as benefitting your physical health; we will discuss this further.

- Buy Seasonal Produce

  By purchasing seasonal fruits and vegetables, you are guaranteed fresher and tastier produce that is full of vitamins, with no artificial processes involved. You will find much higher-quality produce at a farmers' market than in a regular supermarket. By consuming seasonal produce, you will avoid producing any energy by burning fossil fuels, which are used for the transportation of food. This therefore reduces your environmental impact.

- Consider Animal By-products a Luxury

  If we consider meat, fish and diary as luxury products (as they were once considered, a long time ago), we can employ a much healthier diet, based predominantly on fruits, grains, and vegetables. By consuming a lower quantity (but greater quality) of animal-derived foods, we would not only be benefitting the animals and the planet, but also our own health. It is now well-known that the healthiest diets are high in vegetables, fruits, grains, and legumes, and are low in animal by-products. Research studies have found a link between an intake of animal products and several health conditions. By reducing our consumption of diary and meat, we are lowering our risk of diabetes, dementia, heart disease and cancer, among other illnesses.[85] This change will also allow us to buy animal ingredients of better quality and kinder origin; it is a win-win situation. If you feel compelled to take this even further, try shifting your diet towards a vegetarian or vegan one. This will truly make an enormously positive impact; you will save lives every day.

If you are up for the challenge, I would recommend watching *The Game Changer* for an overview of what being vegan means. This inspiring film directed by Oscar-winning documentary filmmaker Louie Psihoyos tells the story of James Wilks, a special forces trainer, on his quest to find the optimal diet for human performance.

Whilst a vegan diet may not be suitable for everyone (depending on the constitution and nutritional needs of each individual), the vast majority of people can thrive on it. As an accessible alternative, a vegetarian diet will always be beneficial to any individual's health.

- If Possible, Grow your Own Produce

  Have you ever grown your own tomatoes or herbs? Do you remember the satisfaction that you felt? Growing your own herbs, fruits, and vegetables can be done even without a large space. It is easy to build your own vertical orchard, which will not only bring healthy produce into your home, but will also bring you a great deal of satisfaction.

- If you have a garden, remember to make it insect friendly.

  Don't use pesticides or herbicides. Plant nectar-rich plants that will attract pollinators like bees, favoring native plants. Don't keep your garden overly-manicured; whilst it may look good, it will not house much insect life. According to the National Trust, "long grass is one

of the rarest garden habitats. By letting some or all of your lawn grow, you will make space for many plant and insect species, including butterflies and wildflowers. Mowing the lawn only once every four weeks gives 'short-grass' plants like daisies and white clover a chance to flower in profusion, boosting nectar production tenfold."

There are countless potential benefits if we all make these small changes. We will pressure the system to produce more organic food and fewer genetically-modified products. We will support responsible, green farmers; this effect will allow the soil to heal, making production of goods both tastier and healthier. Factory farms will gradually disappear, ending the suffering of animals and lowering the number of new illnesses related to the consumption of these low-quality animal products. There will be less deforestation due to a lower demand of animal produce, which will consequently help the ecosystem restore itself, allowing the climate to return to stability. By reducing the quantity of crops dedicated to animal consumption, we will contribute to ending world hunger; as previously explained, most of the grains harvested are destined to these animals, not humans. By shifting to a greener agricultural practice, we will regain our health, and return to excellent food quality, full of flavor and nutrients. In this way, we can end much of the suffering on Earth.

Does this all sound too optimistic? Maybe. But union is power, and we all have the power to make change. We just need to be united in our fight for a better world.

5.2 In Fossil Fuels

- Use public transport. If this is not feasible, use your bicycle or walk as much as possible instead of using your car. This will not only help the environment, but will keep you fit and healthy, whilst also saving you money. If this still is not possible, carpool whenever you can, and/or use an energy-efficient car.

- Limit air travel as much as possible. When you travel, try not to jump into an airplane for every journey. Traveling by train or boat is more eco-friendly. Try to increase local vacations and 'staycations'. There are so many beautiful places to be explored close to home. When you travel locally, it is not just environmentally friendly, but is also largely stress-free, and will allow you to support your local economy.

- Use your air conditioning or heating sparingly. During the summer months, open all your windows to generate a breeze of fresh air. You can also install fans that will keep the air refreshed; this will also make any use of air conditioning more effective. An excellent step to take in achieving a greener home and lowering your carbon footprint is to buy eco-friendly AC units. There are several already on the market that will also lower your electricity bills.

  In winter, try to set your heating a few degrees lower than usual. You could also schedule your heating system so that it does not run permanently. Close all windows and doors to avoid heat waste.

- Turn off your lights and electronic devices when not in use. Many people leave the TV on permanently; this is not an eco-friendly practice, and it is not good for your mental wellbeing either. We don't have to be afraid of silence!

- Change to energy-efficient light bulbs. This way, you will also save on your energy bills.

- Air-dry your laundry where possible. This will also extend the lifetime of your clothes.

- When you have to replace an appliance, check that the new one is energy efficient. Most appliances usually have a label that will indicate this.

- If you can afford to do so, and you live in a sunny area, consider installing solar panels to provide some of your energy needs. The initial installation requires a significant investment, but the panels are relatively maintenance-free and last a long time. Over time, you will save money on your electricity bill, also.

- Plant trees if you have the chance; they are the ultimate air purifiers. The more the merrier!

- Reduce your food waste. About one third of all food produced in the world is wasted, and this is mainly in developed countries. To minimize your waste, eat leftovers, and make sure to use all the ingredients that you buy. Create compost for your plants with the organic waste you produce.

- Recycle, recycle, recycle. It takes up to 500 years for plastic to disintegrate in landfills. The fact that most of this plastic – such as plastic grocery bags – is used only once in its lifetime proves just how much margin there is for improvement. Simply carrying a reusable tote when you shop is an important step towards change. In the same way, we could also bring our own reusable cup or mug when buying drinks to take away. These are just a few examples that could make a resounding, positive impact on the environment if done collectively.

  Recycling items such as metals, glass, and plastics reduces the use of natural resources; we are reusing these materials instead of new ones to produce energy. So recycling is a win-win. Not only

does it save valuable energy, but also reduces levels of pollution in the environment. Unfortunately, the recycling system is not yet an efficient practice in most parts of the world. Focusing for a moment upon plastic, India is the winner, recycling about 60% of its plastic waste. In contrast, the USA, one of the countries that generates the most waste, recycles less than 10% of its plastic. All waste that is not recycled ends up in landfills and waterways.

One of the reasons for this low recycling rate is the fact that most waste destined for recycling becomes contaminated, ending up instead in general waste. We can help to increase this figure simply by rinsing our recycled items before depositing them in the recycling bin to avoid contamination. In many countries, there are government web pages which inform its citizens on the correct way to recycle. If you ever find yourself in doubt, you can consult your local government/council website for further guidance on the correct way to recycle in your area.

5.3 In Over-Consumption

- Every time you feel an impulse to buy something, stop and consider whether it is something that you really need.

- If the need is real, try to buy it in a charity shop, or a second-hand shop. You would be surprised at the beautiful and exclusive pieces that you could find!

- When buying in a store, avoid cheap brands, as they are often a sign of non-sustainable manufacturing. You can search the web for affordable sustainable fashion to discover many new brands that you could try. Even if your budget is restricted, it makes more sense to buy a good quality, staple garment that will last much longer than bulk buying.

- Have you heard of upcycling? You can give new life to those garments or materials that you don't use anymore, and cleverly reuse them to create an upcycled item. This can be a lamp, a piece of furniture, or some shorts! With upcycling anything is possible! You can find endless ideas on YouTube videos and bloggers' websites.

- Declutter your home to discover how much unnecessary "stuff" you own, and donate anything unwanted to charity. It will immediately make you feel better.

- Try to recycle and reuse what you already have.

- If you really need something, it is better to buy it from a top-quality shop. This way, it will last a lifetime.

5.4 On Ethics

- Think well of others. Try not to label anybody. Remember that appearances can be deceiving.

- Stay well-informed of new technologies and get involved when you feel that they go against fundamental ethical principles; ideas for involvement can include starting a Change.org petition, or informing others about said new technology and explaining why you think it is unethical, etc.

- No matter your profession, your decisions and actions should always be based upon ethical principles that will benefit - or at least not harm - the lives of others or the environment.

- Do not use your power as a human being to inflict pain and suffering on other forms of life on Earth.

- Research the brands you purchase, assuring they are ethical, e.g., do not practice animal testing.

- Explore GiveWell and The Life you can Save and choose an NGO. It does not matter if your donation is minimal; we all have a moral obligation to help those who are not as lucky as we are.

- Never ignore or judge a homeless person, or someone in need. You don't know his/her circumstances. If you are not willing to help him/her, at least acknowledge their presence. Smile and be kind to them.

5.5 On Yourself

- Live every day in mindful bliss, as if it were your last. The truth is that death can occur at any moment. We must live fully and be present with our five senses.

- Discover yourself, your values, and your true dreams, and act according to that discovery. Don't worry about the opinion of others, and don't compare yourself with anybody but your past self.

- Acknowledge and be grateful for all those things that we take for granted: your health, your family, your job, etc.

- Be optimistic about life and its impermanence.

- Meditate according to your schedule. Gradually, you will become aware of its benefits, and you will consider it a priority in your life.

- Limit the time you spend on social networks.

5.6 Additional Actions for Change

- Stay informed. As we discussed at the beginning of this book, information is key for change. To be able to influence the people around us and to pressure the governments for change, we must keep ourselves informed. We have to know the facts, stay up-to-date with what is happening in our world, and work towards a more sustainable and kinder society.

- Get to know your politicians and vote for those who are greener and more environmentally-conscious. Familiarize yourself with environmental laws and new regulations in your local area. Get involved and put pressure on your leaders to take important steps in order to protect nature.

- Speak up. Talk about the environment with your friends, family, and co-workers. Post on your social media platforms to inform your followers. In a discreet but confident manner, inform the world, and encourage them to make positive changes for the planet. I am sure that many people are not aware of the levels of damage that we are causing to the world, and would make an immediate positive change if informed.

- Support greener brands and avoid irresponsible ones. Use your power as a consumer to support companies that do good to the environment and to humanity. Patagonia and Eillen Fisher apparel brands, as well as Toms, Allbirds, and Greats footwear are all good examples of sustainable companies. For personal care, Honest, Welleda, and Tisserand are some green brands that you can trust. For cleaning products, Method Home in the US or Clean Living in the UK are excellent choices; related to food, Numi Tea, Alpro, or Oneearth Organics are all sustainable and responsible brands that are better for the earth and for yourself.[86] Focusing now upon pollution, companies such as Coca Cola, closely followed by Pepsico and Nestle, find themselves at the top of the naughty list, producing the largest quantities of plastic waste.[87] The good news is that these companies are feeling the pressure from consumers, and are now investing in adopting greener policies and processes. All three companies are part of the NaturALL Bottle Alliance: a research consortium whose goal is the development of packaging made from 100% sustainable and renewable resources.

- Be an online and offline activist. As Author Naomi Klein demonstrates in her book *This Changes Everything*, it is up to us, the regular citizens, to make THE change, because our leaders are not doing so.[88] We must join the Climate Movement, be part of Extinction Rebellion. We have to sign petitions, march together for the planet, spread important information on social media, always making sure of its trustful and reliable source; as we saw earlier, it is vital to confirm our sources so there is no doubt that the data and facts we share are true. We must carefully choose and support NGO organizations such as Greenpeace that are working hard for the planet.[89]

CONCLUSION

 Whatever affects one directly, affects all indirectly. I can never be what I ought to be until you are what you ought to be. This is the interrelated structure of reality.

- MARTIN LUTHER KING, JR.

L ife was forced to come to a standstill in a number of countries across the globe when the COVID-19 pandemic struck. This global impasse has affected nearly every country around the world, making us realize just how connected we truly are. Perhaps a drastic event such as this was necessary to make us wake up and think further about the detrimental effects of our activities on Earth, and about our egocentric vision of life. With any luck, this might bring a positive change within us all to protect nature and its ecosystems: a change that is absolutely necessary to saving our planet. With a pause in the economy and in our everyday lives, we began to realize that most of what we produce, all those material "things" we think we need, and which cause such harm to the environment, are not essential. What is essential is the very thing we are destroying: the air and the water, the earth and the sky. What we truly missed during the time spent in lockdown were our loved ones.

Is this recent pandemic going to allow us to reflect upon our lives? To see how we are all interconnected? To make us appreciate that the important things do not come from the materialistic world? What matters is our health, our family and friends, nature, and all forms of life. Maybe it is a spiritual message, sent to urge us all to consider what truly matters, and start changing our attitudes towards life.

Within the pages of this book, we have explored the interconnection among us all, and how every action has a reaction that goes much further than we may expect. We are now aware of the destruction that the Anthropocene Era is causing to our planet, and to all living beings on Earth; we are aware that the national, local, and economic interests of most large multinational corporations, politicians, and leaders clash with the greener and more altruistic policies that we so urgently need.

We cannot continue to waste time playing God with new technological solutions that could further damage the planet. With the global halt around the world, we have seen that nature can rebound if we give it a chance – if we don't wait any longer to act up and support it. But it is up to each one of us to do something about this. Passivity is no longer acceptable; we need unity and pro-action from every one of us to save the earth and gain justice for those most affected by its degradation. Humanity has to realize that the earth does not need us, but that we need her. We have to respect her and take care of her. We are her guests; she is not ours to exploit.

We are now aware that we don't have to wait for our leaders to make a change: we ourselves have the power to create a more ethical world, with unity, knowledge and self-transformation at its core. We have seen that we can all make changes in our lives that can modify the path to disaster that we are currently following. It is time for altruism, unity, and compassion, for thinking of others more than oneself. It is time to appreciate the connection between us all, as the welfare of others directly affects our own. It is time to return to our principles, ethics, and real values; to place them where they belong, at the center of our decisions. Now more than ever, our voice can be heard from every corner of the earth. Social media is on our side, helping us reach out to as many people as possible. We can encourage others to join the Pacific Revolution towards a healthier planet and a kinder world. Together, this can be done.

We all have the potential to offer kindness to all beings wherever we go, and this should be our goal in life. When we have an open heart, we begin to think more about the wellbeing of the other, distancing ourselves from our tyrannic ego and thus forgetting about the suffering created by our own mind. By helping our neighbor, we are helping ourselves. Altruism and compassion are the only paths to saving the earth and all its inhabitants: the only path to true happiness. As Douglas Abrams concludes in *The Book of Joy*:

"The more we turned away from our self-regards to wipe the tears from the eyes of another, the more-incredibly we are able to bear, to heal, and to transcend our own suffering. This was their true secret to joy."[90]

BIBLIOGRAPHY BY CHAPTER

CHAPTER 1

1   Wohlleben, Peter, *The Secret Network of Nature: The Delicate Balance of All Living Things* (Vintage, 2017).

2   Wohlleben, Peter.

3   Myriam Preuss et al., "Low Childhood Nature Exposure Is Associated with Worse Mental Health in Adulthood," *International Journal of Environmental Research and Public Health* 16, no. 10 (May 22, 2019): 1809, https://doi.org/10.3390/ijerph16101809.

4   Preuss et al.

5   "Living Planet Report 2020," WWF, September 9, 2020, https://www.wwf.org.uk/press-release/living-planet-report-2020.

6   Emma Pelton, "Early Thanksgiving Counts Show a Critically Low Monarch Population in California," *Xerces Society for Invertebrate Conservation* (blog), November 29, 2018, https://xerces.org/blog/early-thanksgiving-counts-show-critically-low-monarch-population-in-california.

7   "Predictions of Future Global Climate | UCAR Center for Science Education," accessed November 17, 2020, https://scied.ucar.edu/learning-zone/impacts-climate-change/predictions-future-global-climate.

8   Eric Wolff et al., "Climate Change: Evidence & Causes 2020" (The Royal Society, 2020), https://royalsociety.org/-/media/Royal_Society_Content/policy/projects/climate-evidence-causes/climate-change-evidence-causes.pdf.

9   "WHO | Climate Change," WHO (World Health Organization), accessed November 17, 2020, https://www.who.int/heli/risks/climate/climatechange/en/.

10 David Quammen, "We Made the Coronavirus Epidemic," *The New York Times*, January 28, 2020, sec. Opinion, https://www.nytimes.com/2020/01/28/opinion/coronavirus-china.html.

11 Tyler Clevenger and Matt Herbert, "7 Ways the Trump Administration Is Harming the Climate," World Resources Institute, April 21, 2020, https://www.wri.org/blog/2020/04/7-ways-trump-administration-harming-climate.

12 "China | Climate Action Tracker," Climate Action Tracker, accessed November 17, 2020, https://climateactiontracker.org/countries/china/.

13 Letícia Casado and Ernesto Londoño, "Under Brazil's Far-Right Leader, Amazon Protections Slashed and Forests Fall (Published 2019)," *The New York Times*, July 28, 2019, sec. World, https://www.nytimes.com/2019/07/28/world/americas/brazil-deforestation-amazon-bolsonaro.html.

14 Maria Laura Canineu and Andrea Carvalho, "Bolsonaro's Plan to Legalize Crimes Against Indigenous Peoples," Human Rights Watch, March 1, 2020, https://www.hrw.org/news/2020/03/01/bolsonaros-plan-legalize-crimes-against-indigenous-peoples.

15 Colin Ockleford et al., "Scientific Opinion of the PPR Panel on the Follow-up of the Findings of the External Scientific Report 'Literature Review of Epidemiological Studies Linking Exposure to Pesticides and Health Effects' - - 2017 - EFSA Journal - Wiley Online Library," *EFSA Journal* 15, no. 10 (October 31, 2017), https://efsa.onlinelibrary.wiley.com/doi/10.2903/j.efsa.2017.5007.

16 "Dirt Poor: Have Fruits and Vegetables Become Less Nutritious?," Scientific American, April 27, 2011, https://www.scientificamerican.com/article/soil-depletion-and-nutrition-loss/.

17 Simranjeet Singh et al., "Glyphosate Uptake, Translocation, Resistance Emergence in Crops, Analytical Monitoring, Toxicity and Degradation: A Review," *Environmental Chemistry Letters* 18, no. 3 (February 15, 2020): 663–702, https://doi.org/10.1007/s10311-020-00969-z.

18 Gopal Tiwari et al., "Soil Biodiversity: Status, Indicators and Threats," *Biotica Research Today* 2, no. 5 Spl. (May 28, 2020): 353–55.

19 Josh Sager, "From Agent Orange to Pesticides and Genetically Engineered Crops. Why Not to Trust Monsanto," Global Research, May 26, 2013, https://www.globalresearch.ca/from-agent-orange-to-pesticides-and-genetically-engineered-crops-why-not-to-trust-monsanto/5336444.

20 Jonathan R. Latham, "GMO Dangers: Facts You Need to Know - Center for Nutrition Studies," CNS, August 14, 2015, https://nutritionstudies.org/gmo-dangers-facts-you-need-to-know/.

21 Gabriella Andreotti et al., "Glyphosate Use and Cancer Incidence in the Agricultural Health Study," *JNCI: Journal of the National Cancer Institute* 110, no. 5 (May 1, 2018): 509–16, https://doi.org/10.1093/jnci/djx233.

22 Laura N Vandenberg et al., "Is It Time to Reassess Current Safety Standards for Glyphosate-Based Herbicides? | Journal of Epidemiology & Community Health," *J Epidemiol Community Health* 71, no. 6 (2017), https://jech.bmj.com/content/71/6/613.

23 "Veterans and Agent Orange: Health Effects of Herbicides Used in Vietnam" (The National Academics of Science Engineering Medicine, 1994), https://doi.org/10.17226/2141.

24 "Monsanto's Dirty Dozen. Twelve Products That Monsanto Has Brought to Market," Global Research, July 25, 2016, https://www.globalresearch.ca/monsantos-dirty-dozen-twelve-products-that-monsanto-has-brought-to-market/5537809.

25 Doug Gurian-Sherman, "Failure to Yield: Evaluating the Performance of Genetically Engineered Crops" (Union of Concerned Scientists, July 2009), https://www.ucsusa.org/sites/default/files/2019-10/failure-to-yield.pdf.

26 Brian Tokar, "The GMO Threat to Food Sovereignty: Science, Resistance and Transformation" (Praeger, January 1, 2014), Brian Tokar.

27 Francisco Sánchez-Bayo and Kris A. G. Wyckhuys, "Worldwide Decline of the Entomofauna: A Review of Its Drivers," *Biological Conservation* 232 (April 1, 2019): 8–27, https://doi.org/10.1016/j.biocon.2019.01.020.

28 "Monsanto's Dirty Dozen. Twelve Products That Monsanto Has Brought to Market."

29 Jeff McMahon, "Meat and Agriculture Are Worse for The Climate Than Power Generation, Steven Chu Says," *EPIC | Energy Policy Institute at the University of Chicago* (blog), April 4, 2019, https://epic.uchicago.edu/news/meat-and-agriculture-are-worse-for-the-climate-than-power-generation-steven-chu-says/.

30 Madhur S. Dhingra et al., "Geographical and Historical Patterns in the Emergences of Novel Highly Pathogenic Avian Influenza (HPAI) H5 and H7 Viruses in Poultry," *Frontiers in Veterinary Science* 5 (2018), https://doi.org/10.3389/fvets.2018.00084.

31 Jacy Reese Anthis, "US Factory Farming Estimates," *Sentience Institute*, Estimates, April 11, 2019, https://sentienceinstitute.org/us-factory-farming-estimates.

32 Dhingra et al., "Geographical and Historical Patterns in the Emergences of Novel Highly Pathogenic Avian Influenza (HPAI) H5 and H7 Viruses in Poultry."

33 Graham Readfearn, "More than 80% of Indian Ocean Dolphins May Have Been Killed by Commercial Fishing, Study Finds," The Guardian, March 2, 2020, http://www.theguardian.com/environment/2020/mar/03/more-than-80-of-indian-ocean-dolphins-may-have-been-killed-by-commercial-fishing-study-finds.

34 "RSPO - Search for Members," accessed November 17, 2020, https://rspo.org/members/search-for-members.

35 "Earth Overshoot Day 2020," Earth Overshoot Day, accessed November 20, 2020, https://www.overshootday.org/.

36 "Discover the Plastic Islands That Pollute Our Oceans," Iberdrola, accessed November 20, 2020, https://www.iberdrola.com/environment/5-garbage-patches-in-the-ocean.

37 Anna Szyniszewska, "Invasive Species and Climate Change," accessed November 20, 2020, http://climate.org/archive/topics/ecosystems/invasivespecies.html.

38 Ian Tucker, "The Five: Ways That Fashion Threatens the Planet | Fashion Industry | The Guardian," The Guardian, June 23, 2019, https://www.theguardian.com/fashion/2019/jun/23/five-ways-fashion-damages-the-planet.

CHAPTER II

39 "Henri Tajfel's Research Works | University of Bristol, Bristol (UB) and Other Places," accessed May 23, 2021, https://www.researchgate.net/scientific-contributions/Henri-Tajfel-2032190402.

40 Eric Young, "How Millennials Get News: Inside the Habits of America's First Digital Generation," American Press Institute, March 2015, 40.

41 Sarah Evanega et al., "Coronavirus Misinformation: Quantifying Sources and Themes in the COVID-19 'Infodemic,'" 2020, 13.

42 Neil Hawkes, "Does Teaching Values Improve the Quality of Education in Primary Schools?" (http://purl.org/dc/dcmitype/Text, University of Oxford, 2005), https://ora.ox.ac.uk/objects/uuid:bdb77d49-ab71-4d2b-87eb-ffa040ade219.

43 Daniel Kahneman and Angus Deaton, "High Income Improves Evaluation of

Life but Not Emotional Well-Being," *COGNITIVE SCIENCES*, August 4, 2010, 5.

44 Liz Mineo, "Good Genes Are Nice, but Joy Is Better," *The Harvard Gazette* (blog), April 11, 2017, https://news.harvard.edu/gazette/story/2017/04/over-nearly-80-years-harvard-study-has-been-showing-how-to-live-a-healthy-and-happy-life/.

45 "Anti-Muslim Assaults at Highest Level since 2001," *Pew Research Center* (blog), November 21, 2016, https://www.pewresearch.org/wp-content/uploads/2016/11/FT_16.11.21_muslimHateCrimes.png.

46 Griffin Sims Edwards and Stephen Rushin, "The Effect of President Trump's Election on Hate Crimes," SSRN Scholarly Paper (Rochester, NY: Social Science Research Network, January 31, 2019), https://doi.org/10.2139/ssrn.3102652.

47 "FBI: 2018 Hate Crime Statistics," FBI: UCR, accessed November 22, 2020, https://ucr.fbi.gov/hate-crime/2018/hate-crime.

CHAPTER III

48 Ashley Crossman, "Sociological Explanations of Deviant Behavior," ThoughtCo., July 14, 2019, https://www.thoughtco.com/sociological-explanations-of-deviant-behavior-3026269.

49 "About Stem Cells," Cryo Cell International, accessed November 22, 2020, https://www.cryo-cell.com/cord-blood/about-stem-cells.

50 Marcin Wysoczynski and Roberto Bolli, "A Realistic Appraisal of the Use of Embryonic Stem Cell-Based Therapies for Cardiac Repair," *European Heart Journal* 41, no. 25 (July 1, 2020): 2397–2404, https://doi.org/10.1093/eurheartj/ehz787.

51 Max Roser, Esteban Ortiz-Ospina, and Hannah Ritchie, "Life Expectancy," *Our World in Data*, October 2019, https://ourworldindata.org/life-expectancy.

52 Ben Goldacre, *Bad Pharma: How Drug Companies Mislead Doctors and Harm Patients* (London: Fourth Estate, 2012).

53 Sean Rayford, "Medical Devices Have Caused More than 80,000 Deaths since 2008- STAT," STAT News, November 25, 2018, https://www.statnews.com/2018/11/25/medical-devices-pain-other-conditions-more-than-80000-deaths-since-2008/.

54 Peter C. Gøtzsche, *Survival in an Overmedicated World: Look Up the Evidence Yourself* (Art People, 2019).

55 Katherine D. McManus, MS, RD LDN, "10 Superfoods to Boost a Healthy Diet," Harvard Health Blog, 2020, https://www.health.harvard.edu/blog/10-superfoods-to-boost-a-healthy-diet-2018082914463.

56 "A Simple Spice That May Battle Cancer," *John Hopkins Health*, July 16, 2013, https://www.hopkinsmedicine.org/news/publications/johns_hopkins_health/summer_2013/a_simple_spice_that_may_battle_cancer.

57 Martin A. Makary and Michael Daniel, "Medical Error—the Third Leading Cause of Death in the US," *BMJ* 353 (May 3, 2016), https://doi.org/10.1136/bmj.i2139.

58 *Taking Action Against Clinician Burnout A Systems Approach to Professional Well-Being* (Washington, DC: The National Academies Press, 2019).

59 Rolnei R. Daros et al., "Separation from the Dam Causes Negative Judgement Bias in Dairy Calves," *PLOS ONE* 9, no. 5 (May 21, 2014): e98429, https://doi.org/10.1371/journal.pone.0098429.

60 J. L. Edgar et al., "Avian Maternal Response to Chick Distress," *Proceedings of the Royal Society B: Biological Sciences* 278, no. 1721 (October 22, 2011): 3129–34, https://doi.org/10.1098/rspb.2010.2701.

61 Sam Wong, "Ravens' Fear of Unseen Snoopers Hints They Have Theory of Mind," New Scientist, February 2, 2016, https://www.newscientist.com/article/2076025-ravens-fear-of-unseen-snoopers-hints-they-have-theory-of-mind/.

62 J. P. Burkett et al., "Oxytocin-Dependent Consolation Behavior in Rodents," *Science (New York, N.Y.)* 351, no. 6271 (January 22, 2016): 375–78, https://doi.org/10.1126/science.aac4785.

63 M. Boeckle et al., "New Caledonian Crows Plan for Specific Future Tool Use," *Proceedings of the Royal Society B: Biological Sciences* 287, no. 1938 (October 12, 2020): 7, https://doi.org/10.1098/rspb.2020.1490.

64 Sarah Marsh, "The Rise of Vegan Teenagers: 'More People Are into It Because of Instagram,'" The Guardian, May 27, 2016, http://www.theguardian.com/lifeandstyle/2016/may/27/the-rise-of-vegan-teenagers-more-people-are-into-it-because-of-instagram.

65 Priscilla Cohn, "Hunting Myths," 2006, http://istas.net/descargas/Priscilla%20COHN%20Hunting%20Paper%20for%20Madrid.pdf.

66 "Alternatives to Animal Testing and Safety Assessment of Chemicals," Text, EU Science Hub - European Commission, 2017, https://ec.europa.eu/jrc/en/research-topic/alternatives-animal-testing-and-safety-assessment-chemicals.

67 Jabr Ferris, "It's Official: Fish Feel Pain | Science | Smithsonian Magazine," 2018, https://www.smithsonianmag.com/science-nature/fish-feel-pain-180967764/.

68 Peter Singer, *The Life You Can Save*, 10th ed. (Random House, 2010).

69 "The Facts: What You Need to Know About Global Hunger," Mercy Corps, 2020, https://www.mercycorps.org/blog/quick-facts-global-hunger.

70 "Malaria," World Health Organization, 2019, https://www.who.int/newsroom/facts-in-pictures/detail/malaria.

71 Charles G. Gertler et al., "Weakening of the Extratropical Storm Tracks in Solar Geoengineering Scenarios," *Geophysical Research Letters* 47, no. 11 (2020): e2020GL087348, https://doi.org/10.1029/2020GL087348.

72 Gayle Spinazze, "Geoengineering: Worth the Risk?" *Bulletin of the Atomic Scientists* (blog), April 3, 2019, https://thebulletin.org/2019/04/geoengineering-worth-the-risk/.

CHAPTER IV

73 Melissa G. Hunt et al., "No More FOMO: Limiting Social Media Decreases Loneliness and Depression," *Journal of Social and Clinical Psychology* 37, no. 10 (December 2018): 751–68, https://doi.org/10.1521/jscp.2018.37.10.751.

74 Trevor Haynes, "Dopamine, Smartphones & You: A Battle for Your Time," *Science in the News* | *Harvard University* (blog), May 1, 2018, http://sitn.hms.harvard.edu/flash/2018/dopamine-smartphones-battle-time/.

75 Istvan Schreiner and James P. Malcolm, "The Benefits of Mindfulness Meditation: Changes in Emotional States of Depression, Anxiety, and Stress," *Behaviour Change* 25, no. 3 (February 22, 2012): 156–68, https://doi.org/10.1375/bech.25.3.156.

76 Robert Emmons, "Pay It Forward," Greater Good Magazine, June 1, 2007, https://greatergood.berkeley.edu/article/item/pay_it_forward.

77 Daniel Goleman and Richard Davidson, *Altered Traits: Science Reveals How Meditation Changes Your Mind, Brain, and Body* (Avery Publishing, 2017).

78 Camila P. R. A. T. Valim, Lucas M. Marques, and Paulo S. Boggio, "A Positive Emotional-Based Meditation but Not Mindfulness-Based Meditation Improves Emotion Regulation," *Frontiers in Psychology* 10 (2019), https://doi.org/10.3389/fpsyg.2019.00647.

79 Dacher Keltner, Jason Marsh, and Jeremy Adam Smith, *The Compassionate Instinct: The Science of Human Goodness* (W. W. Norton & Company, 2010).

80 Ed Diener and Martin E.P. Seligman, "Very Happy People," *Psychological Science* 13, no. 1 (January 1, 2002): 81–84, https://doi.org/10.1111/1467-9280.00415.

81 Lorenzo Brenna, "Being Compassionate Makes Us Live Longer," LifeGate, September 2, 2015, https://www.lifegate.com/compassion-improves-health.

82 Tania Singer and Olga M. Klimecki, "Empathy and Compassion," *Current Biology* 24, no. 18 (September 22, 2014): R875–78, https://doi.org/10.1016/j.cub.2014.06.054.

83 Olga M. Klimecki et al., "Functional Neural Plasticity and Associated Changes in Positive Affect after Compassion Training," *Cerebral Cortex (New York, N.Y.: 1991)* 23, no. 7 (July 2013): 1552–61, https://doi.org/10.1093/cercor/bhs142.

84 Laura Marie Edinger-Schons, "People with a Sense of Oneness Experience Greater Life Satisfaction: Effect Is Found Regardless of Religion," ScienceDaily, April 11, 2019, https://www.sciencedaily.com/releases/2019/04/190411101803.htm.

CHAPTER V

85 "Animal Products | Health Topics | NutritionFacts.Org," NutritionFacts.org, accessed November 20, 2020, https://nutritionfacts.org/topics/animal-products/.

86 "Brands | Greener Beauty | Cruelty Free & Vegan Beauty," accessed November 20, 2020, https://www.greenerbeauty.com/product-category/brands/.

87 Kirstin Linnenkoper, "Greenpeace Reveals the Top 5 'Worst Polluting Companies,'" Recycling International, October 10, 2018, https://recyclinginternational.com/plastics/greenpeace-reveals-the-top-5-worst-polluting-companies/17483/.

88 Naomi Klein, *This Changes Everything: Capitalism vs. The Climate* (London: Penguin books, 2015).

89 "Extinction Rebellion | Join the Fight Against Climate and Ecological Collapse," Extinction Rebellion, accessed November 20, 2020, https://rebellion.global/.

CONCLUSION

90 Dalai Lama, Desmond Tutu, and Douglas Abrams, *The Book of Joy*, 6th Edition (Cornerstone Publishers, 2016).

BIBLIOGRAPHY

"A Simple Spice That May Battle Cancer." *John Hopkins Health*, July 16, 2013. https://www.hopkinsmedicine.org/news/publications/johns_hopkins_health/summer_2013/a_simple_spice_that_may_battle_cancer.

Cryo Cell International. "About Stem Cells." Accessed November 22, 2020. https://www.cryo-cell.com/cord-blood/about-stem-cells.

EU Science Hub - European Commission. "Alternatives to Animal Testing and Safety Assessment of Chemicals." Text, 2017. https://ec.europa.eu/jrc/en/research-topic/alternatives-animal-testing-and-safety-assessment-chemicals.

Andreotti, Gabriella, Stella Koutros, Jonathan N. Hofmann, Dale P. Sandler, Jay H. Lubin, Charles F. Lynch, Catherine C. Lerro, et al. "Glyphosate Use and Cancer Incidence in the Agricultural Health Study." *JNCI: Journal of the National Cancer Institute* 110, no. 5 (May 1, 2018): 509–16. https://doi.org/10.1093/jnci/djx233.

NutritionFacts.org. "Animal Products | Health Topics | NutritionFacts.Org." Accessed November 20, 2020. https://nutritionfacts.org/topics/animal-products/.

Anthis, Jacy Reese. "US Factory Farming Estimates." *Sentience Institute*, Estimates, April 11, 2019. https://sentienceinstitute.org/us-factory-farming-estimates.

Pew Research Center. "Anti-Muslim Assaults at Highest Level since 2001," November 21, 2016. https://www.pewresearch.org/wp-content/uploads/2016/11/FT_16.11.21_muslimHateCrimes.png.

Boeckle, M., M. Schiestl, A. Frohnwieser, R. Gruber, R. Miller, T. Suddendorf, R. D. Gray, A. H. Taylor, and N. S. Clayton. "New Caledonian Crows Plan for Specific Future Tool Use." *Proceedings of the Royal Society B: Biological Sciences* 287, no. 1938 (October 12, 2020): 7. https://doi.org/10.1098/rspb.2020.1490.

"Brands | Greener Beauty | Cruelty Free & Vegan Beauty." Accessed November 20, 2020. https://www.greenerbeauty.com/product-category/brands/.

Brenna, Lorenzo. "Being Compassionate Makes Us Live Longer." LifeGate, September 2, 2015. https://www.lifegate.com/compassion-improves-health.

Burkett, J. P., E. Andari, Z. V. Johnson, D. C. Curry, F. B. M. de Waal, and L. J. Young. "Oxytocin-Dependent Consolation Behavior in Rodents." *Science (New York, N.Y.)* 351, no. 6271 (January 22, 2016): 375–78. https://doi.org/10.1126/science.aac4785.

Canineu, Maria Laura, and Andrea Carvalho. "Bolsonaro's Plan to Legalize Crimes Against Indigenous Peoples." Human Rights Watch, March 1, 2020. https://www.hrw.org/news/2020/03/01/bolsonaros-plan-legalize-crimes-against-indigenous-peoples.

Casado, Letícia, and Ernesto Londoño. "Under Brazil's Far-Right Leader, Amazon Protections Slashed and Forests Fall (Published 2019)." *The New York Times*, July 28, 2019, sec. World. https://www.nytimes.com/2019/07/28/world/americas/brazil-deforestation-amazon-bolsonaro.html.

Climate Action Tracker. "China | Climate Action Tracker." Accessed November 17, 2020. https://climateactiontracker.org/countries/china/.

Clevenger, Tyler, and Matt Herbert. "7 Ways the Trump Administration Is Harming the Climate." World Resources Institute, April 21, 2020. https://www.wri.org/blog/2020/04/7-ways-trump-administration-harming-climate.

Cohn, Priscilla. "Hunting Myths," 2006. http://istas.net/descargas/Priscilla%20COHN%20Hunting%20Paper%20for%20Madrid.pdf.

Crossman, Ashley. "Sociological Explanations of Deviant Behavior." ThoughtCo., July 14, 2019. https://www.thoughtco.com/sociological-explanations-of-deviant-behavior-3026269.

Daros, Rolnei R., João H. C. Costa, Marina A. G. von Keyserlingk, Maria J. Hötzel, and Daniel M. Weary. "Separation from the Dam Causes Negative Judgement Bias in Dairy Calves." *PLOS ONE* 9, no. 5 (May 21, 2014): e98429. https://doi.org/10.1371/journal.pone.0098429.

Dhingra, Madhur S., Jean Artois, Simon Dellicour, Philippe Lemey, Gwenaelle Dauphin, Sophie Von Dobschuetz, Thomas P. Van Boeckel, David M. Castellan, Subhash Morzaria, and Marius Gilbert. "Geographical and Historical Patterns in the Emergences of Novel Highly Pathogenic Avian Influenza (HPAI) H5 and H7 Viruses in Poultry." *Frontiers in Veterinary Science* 5 (2018). https://doi.org/10.3389/fvets.2018.00084.

Diener, Ed, and Martin E.P. Seligman. "Very Happy People." *Psychological Science* 13, no. 1 (January 1, 2002): 81–84. https://doi.org/10.1111/1467-9280.00415.

Scientific American. "Dirt Poor: Have Fruits and Vegetables Become Less Nutritious?" April 27, 2011. https://www.scientificamerican.com/article/soil-depletion-and-nutrition-loss/.

Iberdrola. "Discover the Plastic Islands That Pollute Our Oceans." Accessed November 20, 2020. https://www.iberdrola.com/environment/5-garbage-patches-in-the-ocean.

Earth Overshoot Day. "Earth Overshoot Day 2020." Accessed November 20, 2020. https://www.overshootday.org/.

Edgar, J. L., J. C. Lowe, E. S. Paul, and C. J. Nicol. "Avian Maternal Response to Chick Distress." *Proceedings of the Royal Society B: Biological Sciences* 278, no. 1721 (October 22, 2011): 3129–34. https://doi.org/10.1098/rspb.2010.2701.

Edinger-Schons, Laura Marie. "People with a Sense of Oneness Experience Greater Life Satisfaction: Effect Is Found Regardless of Religion." ScienceDaily, April 11, 2019. https://www.sciencedaily.com/releases/2019/04/190411101803.htm.

Edwards, Griffin Sims, and Stephen Rushin. "The Effect of President Trump's Election on Hate Crimes." SSRN Scholarly Paper. Rochester, NY: Social Science Research Network, January 31, 2019. https://doi.org/10.2139/ssrn.3102652.

Emmons, Robert. "Pay It Forward." Greater Good Magazine, June 1, 2007. https://greatergood.berkeley.edu/article/item/pay_it_forward.

Evanega, Sarah, Mark Lynas, Jordan Adams, and Karinne Smolenyak. "Coronavirus Misinformation: Quantifying Sources and Themes in the COVID-19 'Infodemic,'" 2020, 13.

Extinction Rebellion. "Extinction Rebellion | Join the Fight Against Climate and Ecological Collapse." Accessed November 20, 2020. https://rebellion.global/.

FBI: UCR. "FBI: 2018 Hate Crime Statistics." Accessed November 22, 2020. https://ucr.fbi.gov/hate-crime/2018/hate-crime.

Ferris, Jabr. "It's Official: Fish Feel Pain | Science | Smithsonian Magazine," 2018. https://www.smithsonianmag.com/science-nature/fish-feel-pain-180967764/.

Gertler, Charles G., Paul A. O'Gorman, Ben Kravitz, John C. Moore, Steven J. Phipps, and Shingo Watanabe. "Weakening of the Extratropical Storm Tracks in Solar Geoengineering Scenarios." *Geophysical Research Letters* 47, no. 11 (2020): e2020GL087348. https://doi.org/10.1029/2020GL087348.

Goldacre, Ben. *Bad Pharma: How Drug Companies Mislead Doctors and Harm Patients.* London: Fourth Estate, 2012.

Goleman, Daniel, and Richard Davidson. *Altered Traits: Science Reveals How Meditation Changes Your Mind, Brain, and Body.* Avery Publishing, 2017.

Gøtzsche, Peter C. *Survival in an Overmedicated World: Look Up the Evidence Yourself.* Art People, 2019.

Gurian-Sherman, Doug. "Failure to Yield: Evaluating the Performance of Genetically Engineered Crops." Union of Concerned Scientists, July 2009. https://www.ucsusa.org/sites/default/files/2019-10/failure-to-yield.pdf.

Hawkes, Neil. "Does Teaching Values Improve the Quality of Education in Primary Schools?" Http://purl.org/dc/dcmitype/Text, University of Oxford, 2005. https://ora.ox.ac.uk/objects/uuid:bdb77d49-ab71-4d2b-87eb-ffa040ade219.

Haynes, Trevor. "Dopamine, Smartphones & You: A Battle for Your Time." *Science in the News | Harvard University* (blog), May 1, 2018. http://sitn.hms.harvard.edu/flash/2018/dopamine-smartphones-battle-time/.

"Henri Tajfel's Research Works | University of Bristol, Bristol (UB) and Other Places." Accessed May 23, 2021. https://www.researchgate.net/scientific-contributions/Henri-Tajfel-2032190402.

Hunt, Melissa G., Rachel Marx, Courtney Lipson, and Jordyn Young. "No More FOMO: Limiting Social Media Decreases Loneliness and Depression." *Journal of Social and Clinical Psychology* 37, no. 10 (December 2018): 751–68. https://doi.org/10.1521/jscp.2018.37.10.751.

Kahneman, Daniel, and Angus Deaton. "High Income Improves Evaluation of Life but Not Emotional Well-Being." *COGNITIVE SCIENCES*, August 4, 2010, 5.

Keltner, Dacher, Jason Marsh, and Jeremy Adam Smith. *The Compassionate Instinct: The Science of Human Goodness.* W. W. Norton & Company, 2010.

Klein, Naomi. *This Changes Everything: Capitalism vs. The Climate.* London: Penguin books, 2015.

Klimecki, Olga M., Susanne Leiberg, Claus Lamm, and Tania Singer. "Functional Neural Plasticity and Associated Changes in Positive Affect after Compassion Training." *Cerebral Cortex (New York, N.Y.: 1991)* 23, no. 7 (July 2013): 1552–61. https://doi.org/10.1093/cercor/bhs142.

Lama, Dalai, Desmond Tutu, and Douglas Abrams. *The Book of Joy.* 6th Edition. Cornerstone Publishers, 2016.

Latham, Jonathan R. "GMO Dangers: Facts You Need to Know - Center for Nutrition Studies." CNS, August 14, 2015. https://nutritionstudies.org/gmo-dangers-facts-you-need-to-know/.

Linnenkoper, Kirstin. "Greenpeace Reveals the Top 5 'Worst Polluting Companies.'" Recycling International, October 10, 2018. https://recyclinginternational.com/plastics/greenpeace-reveals-the-top-5-worst-polluting-companies/17483/.

WWF. "Living Planet Report 2020," September 9, 2020. https://www.wwf.org.uk/press-release/living-planet-report-2020.

Makary, Martin A., and Michael Daniel. "Medical Error—the Third Leading Cause of Death in the US." *BMJ* 353 (May 3, 2016). https://doi.org/10.1136/bmj.i2139.

World Health Organization. "Malaria," 2019. https://www.who.int/news-room/facts-in-pictures/detail/malaria.

Marsh, Sarah. "The Rise of Vegan Teenagers: 'More People Are into It Because of Instagram.'" The Guardian, May 27, 2016. http://www.theguardian.com/lifeandstyle/2016/may/27/the-rise-of-vegan-teenagers-more-people-are-into-it-because-of-instagram.

McMahon, Jeff. "Meat And Agriculture Are Worse for The Climate Than Power Generation, Steven Chu Says." *EPIC | Energy Policy Institute at the University of Chicago* (blog), April 4, 2019. https://epic.uchicago.edu/news/meat-and-agriculture-are-worse-for-the-climate-than-power-generation-steven-chu-says/.

McManus, MS, RD LDN, Katherine D. "10 Superfoods to Boost a Healthy Diet." Harvard Health Blog, 2020. https://www.health.harvard.edu/blog/10-superfoods-to-boost-a-healthy-diet-2018082914463.

Mineo, Liz. "Good Genes Are Nice, but Joy Is Better." *The Harvard Gazette* (blog), April 11, 2017. https://news.harvard.edu/gazette/story/2017/04/over-nearly-80-years-harvard-study-has-been-showing-how-to-live-a-healthy-and-happy-life/.

Global Research. "Monsanto's Dirty Dozen. Twelve Products That Monsanto Has Brought to Market," July 25, 2016. https://www.globalresearch.ca/monsantos-dirty-dozen-twelve-products-that-monsanto-has-brought-to-market/5537809.

Ockleford, Colin, Paulien Adriaanse, Philippe Berny, Theodorus Brock, and Sabine Duquesne. "Scientific Opinion of the PPR Panel on the Follow-up of the Findings of the External Scientific Report 'Literature Review of Epidemiological Studies Linking Exposure to Pesticides and Health Effects' -- 2017 - EFSA Journal - Wiley Online Library." *EFSA Journal* 15, no. 10 (October 31, 2017). https://efsa.onlinelibrary.wiley.com/doi/10.2903/j.efsa.2017.5007.

Pelton, Emma. "Early Thanksgiving Counts Show a Critically Low Monarch Population in California." *Xerces Society for Invertebrate Conservation* (blog), November 29, 2018. https://xerces.org/blog/early-thanksgiving-counts-show-critically-low-monarch-population-in-california.

"Predictions of Future Global Climate | UCAR Center for Science Education." Accessed November 17, 2020. https://scied.ucar.edu/learning-zone/impacts-climate-change/predictions-future-global-climate.

Preuss, Myriam, Mark Nieuwenhuijsen, Sandra Marquez, Marta Cirach, Payam Dadvand, Margarita Triguero-Mas, Christopher Gidlow, Regina Grazuleviciene, Hanneke Kruize, and Wilma Zijlema. "Low Childhood Nature Exposure Is Associated with Worse Mental Health in Adulthood." *International Journal of Environmental Research and Public Health* 16, no. 10 (May 22, 2019): 1809. https://doi.org/10.3390/ijerph16101809.

Quammen, David. "We Made the Coronavirus Epidemic." *The New York Times*, January 28, 2020, sec. Opinion. https://www.nytimes.com/2020/01/28/opinion/coronavirus-china.html.

Rayford, Sean. "Medical Devices Have Caused More than 80,000 Deaths since 2008- STAT." STAT News, November 25, 2018. https://www.statnews.com/2018/11/25/medical-devices-pain-other-conditions-more-than-80000-deaths-since-2008/.

Readfearn, Graham. "More than 80% of Indian Ocean Dolphins May Have Been Killed by Commercial Fishing, Study Finds." The Guardian, March 2, 2020. http://www.theguardian.com/environment/2020/mar/03/more-than-80-of-indian-ocean-dolphins-may-have-been-killed-by-commercial-fishing-study-finds.

Roser, Max, Esteban Ortiz-Ospina, and Hannah Ritchie. "Life Expectancy." *Our World in Data*, October 2019. https://ourworldindata.org/life-expectancy.

"RSPO - Search for Members." Accessed November 17, 2020. https://rspo.org/members/search-for-members.

Sager, Josh. "From Agent Orange to Pesticides and Genetically Engineered Crops. Why Not to Trust Monsanto." Global Research, May 26, 2013. https://www.globalresearch.ca/from-agent-orange-to-pesticides-and-genetically-engineered-crops-why-not-to-trust-monsanto/5336444.

Sánchez-Bayo, Francisco, and Kris A. G. Wyckhuys. "Worldwide Decline of the Entomofauna: A Review of Its Drivers." *Biological Conservation* 232 (April 1, 2019): 8–27. https://doi.org/10.1016/j.biocon.2019.01.020.

Schreiner, Istvan, and James P. Malcolm. "The Benefits of Mindfulness Meditation: Changes in Emotional States of Depression, Anxiety, and Stress." *Behaviour Change* 25, no. 3 (February 22, 2012): 156–68. https://doi.org/10.1375/bech.25.3.156.

Singer, Peter. *The Life You Can Save*. 10th ed. Random House, 2010.

Singer, Tania, and Olga M. Klimecki. "Empathy and Compassion." *Current Biology* 24, no. 18 (September 22, 2014): R875–78. https://doi.org/10.1016/j.cub.2014.06.054.

Singh, Simranjeet, Vijay Kumar, Shivika Datta, Abdul Basit Wani, Daljeet Singh Dhanjal, Romina Romero, and Joginder Singh. "Glyphosate Uptake, Translocation, Resistance Emergence in Crops, Analytical Monitoring, Toxicity and Degradation: A Review." *Environmental Chemistry Letters* 18, no. 3 (February 15, 2020): 663–702. https://doi.org/10.1007/s10311-020-00969-z.

Spinazze, Gayle. "Geoengineering: Worth the Risk?" *Bulletin of the Atomic Scientists* (blog), April 3, 2019. https://thebulletin.org/2019/04/geoengineering-worth-the-risk/.

Szyniszewska, Anna. "Invasive Species and Climate Change." Accessed November 20, 2020. http://climate.org/archive/topics/ecosystems/invasivespecies.html.

Taking Action Against Clinician Burnout A Systems Approach to Professional Well-Being. Washington, DC: The National Academies Press, 2019.

Mercy Corps. "The Facts: What You Need to Know About Global Hunger," 2020. https://www.mercycorps.org/blog/quick-facts-global-hunger.

Tiwari, Gopal, Abhishek Jangir, Lal Chand Malav, and Sandeep Kumar. "Soil Biodiversity: Status, Indicators and Threats." *Biotica Research Today* 2, no. 5 Spl. (May 28, 2020): 353–55.

Tokar, Brian. "The GMO Threat to Food Sovereignty: Science, Resistance and Transformation." Praeger, January 1, 2014. Brian Tokar.

Tucker, Ian. "The Five: Ways That Fashion Threatens the Planet | Fashion Industry | The Guardian." The Guardian, June 23, 2019. https://www.theguardian.com/fashion/2019/jun/23/five-ways-fashion-damages-the-planet.

Valim, Camila P. R. A. T., Lucas M. Marques, and Paulo S. Boggio. "A Positive Emotional-Based Meditation but Not Mindfulness-Based Meditation Improves Emotion Regulation." *Frontiers in Psychology* 10 (2019). https://doi.org/10.3389/fpsyg.2019.00647.

Vandenberg, Laura N, Bruce Blumberg, Michael N Antoniou, Charles M Benbrook, Lynn Carroll, Theo Colborn, Lorne G Everett, et al. "Is It Time to Reassess Current Safety Standards for Glyphosate-Based Herbicides? | Journal of Epidemiology & Community Health." *J Epidemiol Community Health* 71, no. 6 (2017). https://jech.bmj.com/content/71/6/613.

"Veterans and Agent Orange: Health Effects of Herbicides Used in Vietnam." The National Academics of Science Engineering Medicine, 1994. https://doi.org/10.17226/2141.

WHO "WHO | Climate Change." World Health Organization. Accessed November 17, 2020. https://www.who.int/heli/risks/climate/climatechange/en/.

Wohlleben, Peter. *The Secret Network of Nature: The Delicate Balance of All Living Things*. Vintage, 2017.

Wolff, Eric, John Shepherd, Inez Fung, and Keith Shine. "Climate Change: Evidence & Causes 2020." The Royal Society, 2020. https://royalsociety.org/-/media/Royal_Society_Content/policy/projects/climate-evidence-causes/climate-change-evidence-causes.pdf.

Wong, Sam. "Ravens' Fear of Unseen Snoopers Hints They Have Theory of Mind." New Scientist, February 2, 2016. https://www.newscientist.com/article/2076025-ravens-fear-of-unseen-snoopers-hints-they-have-theory-of-mind/.

Wysoczynski, Marcin, and Roberto Bolli. "A Realistic Appraisal of the Use of Embryonic Stem Cell-Based Therapies for Cardiac Repair." *European Heart Journal* 41, no. 25 (July 1, 2020): 2397–2404. https://doi.org/10.1093/eurheartj/ehz787.

Young, Eric. "How Millennials Get News: Inside the Habits of America's First Digital Generation." *American Press Institute*, March 2015, 40.

FURTHER READING

Anderson, Alison, Marianne Dresser, and Dalai Lama. 1996. *Beyond Dogma: Dialogues and Discourses*. Berkeley, California: North Atlantic Books.

André, Christophe, Alexandre Jollien, and Matthieu Ricard. 2018. *Trois amis en quête de sagesse: Un moine, un philosophe, un psychiatre nous parlent de l'essentiel*.

Aoyama, Shundô. 2015. *Le zen et la vie*. Paris: Albin Michel.

Balcombe, Jonathan. 2011. *Second Nature: The Inner Lives of Animals*. New York: Palgrave Macmillan.

Berners-Lee, Mike. 2019. *There Is No Planet B: A Handbook for the Make or Break Years*. Cambridge; New York, NY: Cambridge University Press.

Brownlee, Shannon. 2008. *Overtreated: Why Too Much Medicine Is Making Us Sicker and Poorer*. Pbk. ed. New York, NY: Bloomsbury.

Cousineau, PhD, Tara. 2018. *The Kindness Cure: How the Science of Compassion Can Heal Your Heart and Your World*. Oakland, CA: New Harbinger Publications, Inc.

Dalai Lama. 1995. *El poder de la compasión*. Barcelona: Ediciones Martínez Roca.

Ferrucci, Piero. 2005. *El poder de la bondad: sólo tendremos futuro si pensamos con el corazón*. Urano. Barcelona: Urano.

Figueres, Christiana, and Tom Rivett-Carnac. 2020. *The Future We Choose: Surviving the Climate Crisis*.

Harari, Yuval N. 2018. *21 Lessons for the 21st Century*. London: Penguin Random House UK.

Hopkins, Jeffrey, and Dalai Lama. 2003. *How to Practice: The Way to a Meaningful Life*. New York: Atria Books.

Klein, Naomi. 2015. *This Changes Everything: Capitalism vs. The Climate*. London: Penguin books.

Lama, Dalai. 2005. *The Universe in a Single Atom: The Convergence of Science and Spirituality*. New York: Morgan Road Books.

Lama, Dalai, Desmond Tutu, and Douglas Abrams. 2016. *The Book of Joy: Lasting Happiness in a Changing World*. London: Hutchinson.

Lenoir, Frédéric. 2010. *Petit Traité de Vie Intérieure*. Paris: Plon.

Masson, Jeffrey Moussaieff, and Susan McCarthy. 1996. *When Elephants Weep: The Emotional Lives of Animals*. New York: Delta Trade Paperbacks.

Montgomery, David R. 2018. *Growing a Revolution: Bringing Our Soil Back to Life*.

Nhat Hanh, Thich. 2016. *Silence: The Power of Quiet in a World Full of Noise*.

O'Brien, James. 2018. *How to Be Right: ... In a World Gone Wrong*. WH Allen.

Oreskes, Naomi, and Erik M. Conway. 2011. *Merchants of Doubt: How a Handful of Scientists Obscured the Truth on Issues from Tobacco Smoke to Climate Change*. Paperback edition. New York, NY: Bloomsbury Press.

Piburn, Sidney. 2006. *El Dalai Lama: la política de la bondad: una antología de escritos del y sobre el Dalai Lama*. Novelda: Ediciones Dharma.

Ricard, Matthieu. 2008. *L'art de la méditation*.

———. 2013. *Plaidoyer pour l'altruisme: la force de la bienveillance*. Paris: NIL.

———. 2014. *Plaidoyer pour les animaux: vers une bienveillance pour tous*. http://banq.pretnumerique.ca/accueil/isbn/9782370730299.

Singer, Peter. 2017. *Ethics in the Real World: 82 Brief Essays on Things That Matter*. https://doi.org/10.1515/9781400888733.

———. 2019. *The Life You Can Save: How To Do Your Part To End World Poverty*. 10th Anniversary edition.

The Happy Buddha. 2015. *Mindfulness and Compassion: Embracing Life with Loving-Kindness*. Lewes: Ivy Press.

Wallace-Wells, David. 2019. *The Uninhabitable Earth: Life After Warming*. First edition. New York: Tim Duggan Books.

Watts, Alan. 2003. *Become What You Are*. Expanded ed. Boston: Shambhala.

Wohlleben, Peter, and Jane Billinghurst. 2017. *The Hidden Life of Trees*. William Collins.

———. 2019. *The Secret Network of Nature: The Delicate Balance of All Living Things*.